UNICORN

Praise for *Unicorn*:

'Amrou's story is at times painful, at times hilarious, but always completely resonant. If you've ever felt like an outsider, or caught among several identities, this book is a light in the dark and a soothing balm on the pain of loneliness and alienation'

EMILY V. GORDON & KUMAIL NANJIANI

'This is a masterpiece, an incredible emotional voyage, moving, funny, provocative, educational; a book you must read whatever your ethnicity or your sexual or gender identity. Beautifully written by an author whose voice must be heard'

OWEN JONES, author of *Chavs* and *The Establishment*

'An extraordinarily generous work of compassion, understanding, hope and humour. *Unicorn* is a true gift to all readers – and especially to any hidden unicorns ready and waiting to embrace their magic'

CN LESTER, author of *Trans Like Me*

'Tender and hilarious in equal parts, this is a memoir like no other. A beautiful, honest account of what it is like to grow up between multiple expectations, and an uplifting reminder that it is possible to find happiness by being yourself. I was gripped at every page'

ANGELA SAINI, author of *Superior*

'Raw, emotional: *Unicorn* is a vital and important book. Hilarious, heart-breaking and unquestionably honest, it is a bold account that reminds us that difference is a beautiful necessity in this world'

CHIMENE SULEYMAN, editor of *The Good Immigrant USA*

'*Unicorn* is testament to the bravery required for many queer people to live their truth. This story is our story: one of loneliness, guts, resilience, full-on glamour and wanting to find your people. Amrou writes with emotional intelligence and candour of the eventful journey to a life fully lived. They also know how to deliver a killer one-liner. I wish I'd had this book when I was growing up'

NIVEN GOVINDEN, author of *The Brutal House*

'Like Amrou, this is beautiful, powerful and demands to be heard'

MATTHEW TODD, author of *Straight Jacket* and *Pride*

'Raw, emotional and compelling'   *Stylist*

UNICORN

The Memoir of a Muslim Drag Queen

AMROU AL-KADHI

4th ESTATE • *London*

4th Estate
An imprint of HarperCollins*Publishers*
1 London Bridge Street
London SE1 9GF

www.4thEstate.co.uk

First published in Great Britain in 2019 by 4th Estate

1

A catalogue record for this book is
available from the British Library

ISBN 978-0-00-830606-9 (hardback)
ISBN 978-0-00-830607-6 (trade paperback)

Set in Sabon LT Std
Printed and bound in Great Britain by
CPI Group (UK) Ltd, Croydon

MIX
Paper from
responsible sources
FSC™ C007454

This book is produced from independently certified FSC™ paper
to ensure responsible forest management.

For more information visit: www.harpercollins.co.uk/green

For Queer People
of Colour everywhere
&
Chet & Lois,
my favourite unicorns

For the twenty-fourth night that August, I found myself crossed-legged on the floor of a damp, pungent dressing room. As the rumblings of an Edinburgh crowd reverberated from the venue next door – I say venue, it was more like a cave – I used my little finger to apply gold pigment to my emerald-painted lips. Denim, the drag troupe that I set up seven years earlier, had survived the gruelling Fringe Festival, and we were one show away from crossing our scratched heels over the finish line.

A month of performances, often two a day, had taken its toll. My skin was at war with the industrial quantity of make-up it was being suffocated in (a two-hour procedure each time); I had obliterated my left kneecap because of a wannabe-rockstar 'jump-and-slam-onto-the-ground' move I felt impelled to perform each show; and a boy I was seeing had suddenly disappeared on me (I secretly hoped that death, instead of rejection, would be the explanation, but it turned out he was a ghost of a different sort: *he had indeed stopped fancying me*).

Despite feeling so weathered, I was itching to get onstage again. I always feel empowered when I'm in drag and entertaining a crowd – it's my sanctuary, a space where I invite the audience into my own reality, where I don't need to adhere to the rules of anybody else's. No matter how low I'm feeling, the transformative power of make-up and costume is galvanising; for most of my life I've felt like a failure by male standards, and drag allows me to convert my exterior into an image of defiant femininity. This particular show was always exhilarating to perform, because it was the first time I honestly articulated my tumultuous relationship with Islam onstage, trying to mine humour in the unexpected parallels between being queer and being Muslim. How I haven't been hit with a fatwa yet, I do not know.

A student volunteer usher told us we were moments away from the start of the show, and I did my pre-show ritual where I box with the air and shout 'IT'S GLAMROU, MOTHERFUCKERS'. It comforts me to imagine my haters as the punch bag 'motherfuckers'. Then I formed a circle with my other queens, our hands all joined at the centre in a moment of communion. The synth chords burst through the speakers, and the audience whooped as we strutted through a blackout onto the stage, our backs facing the crowd, pretending that the actual sight of our faces would be some sort of reward. A suspended beat, then lights pummelled the stage. I thrust my arms above me as if it were Wembley (I won't lie; it usually is in my mind), and eyed the dripping condensation coating the cave ceiling, one drop a moment away from plopping on my face. After a prolonged and hyperbolic musical introduction – allow a queen her fifteen minutes – the show began with each of us turning to face the crowd one by one, until I pivoted around last. The next part was supposed to be me proclaiming 'I AM ISLAM', followed by the Muslim call to prayer remixed with Lady Gaga's 'Bad Romance'.

But on this final night, as I opened my mouth to start the show, I felt a little bit of sick at the back of my throat, and I found I couldn't make a sound. Six Muslim women, the majority wearing hijabs, were sitting in the front row. There, looking directly up at me, were multiple avatars of my disapproving mother, about to remind me how shameful I was.

The ensuing performance was about as fun as your parents walking in on you having sex, and then staying to watch until you come. For a section in the show I sang a parodic 'Why-Do-You-Hate-Me' type number to my ex-boyfriend – but the boyfriend I was singing to was Allah. Throughout the routine, the women in front of me were using Allah's name in a more God-fearing way – 'Allah have mercy' (in Arabic) seemed to be the most common refrain. Another highlight included a sketch in which I compare men praying in mosques to gay chemsex orgies.

When I dared glance out in front of me, the mother of the group seemed to be repenting in prayer on my behalf. I started to ricochet around a mental labyrinth of paranoia, the censorious voices from my childhood chattering loudly in my mind. As my past enveloped me, the empowering armour of my drag began to dissolve rapidly. I stumbled over my lines, tripped on my heels – more than once – and even welled up onstage (which caused the eyelash glue to incinerate my cornea). The rest of the drag queens – as well as the audience – were white, so it felt as if the Muslim women and I were operating on a different plane of reality from everyone else, one where only we knew the laws.

Once the show finished, I sprinted backstage and threw up in a bin. My agent knew something was up and ran to the dressing room. I trembled as she hugged me, distressed at the offence I knew I'd caused. I felt like I was fourteen again, when my parents would tell me on a daily basis that my flamboyance was the root of their unhappiness. I'd worked so hard to create my drag utopia, and until that night, it had been my haven.

And then came the news I was dreading. The women, waiting outside the stage door, passed on a message to the usher: they wanted to see me.

Like a reincarnation of my teen-self, I shuffled off outside, with all the strength of a young seahorse adrift on an ocean current. Seven years after drag had liberated me, I was about to relearn that my liberated new identity required disciplinary action.

There they were, all lined up. The mother of the group, who was dressed head to toe in Islamic robes, stared down at the floor, refusing even to look at me. *Great*, I thought, *she thinks I'm Satan*. She whispered something in Arabic to her daughter that I couldn't make out. As her daughter began speaking, I twitched with terror, like a defendant in court about to learn the jury's verdict.

'My mom's super Muslim, yeah, so she's a bit uneasy, but she wanted me to tell you that she thought you were amazing, and that you should be really proud.' *Not guilty*. In my dumbfounded jubilation, I went to hug her mother, who quickly shifted, like a pigeon does when you suddenly kick the pavement.

'Easy, my mom's from Saudi Arabia and really Muslim, so she can't hug you, but she thought it was so cool seeing a gay Muslim on a stage like that. She said she feels really proud to have been here.'

I explained how I believed they were cursing me throughout the show. It turns out their expressions were akin to a colloquial 'Oh my God!' uttered out of enjoyment. The young woman then held my hand, stared honestly into my eyes, and said: 'But your song to Allah ...' *Fuck. Guilty on some counts*. '... it broke my heart. I've been there. Trust me, I've been there – I'm a woman living in Saudi Arabia. But the thing is, Glamrou – Allah loves you.'

And with that, the women said their goodbyes, their Muslim drapery billowing in the Scottish wind, floating away from me like a mystical collective of apparitions, as if the entire encounter might have been a hallucination. Now, in general these days, I find it very difficult to sob – my body rarely gives in to the urge (the only exception being when I watch families in whom I have no investment celebrate their loved ones on X *Factor*, which always gets me). But as the women disappeared from the stage door and into the alleyway leading out to the Edinburgh night, I stepped after them and collapsed against the wall, convulsing so hard that I gave myself a splitting headache. Once the sobbing subsided and I was back out of the matrix, I felt as if I'd emerged from some combination of an exorcism and a K-hole.

I'll forever remember that night as the precise moment when, for the first time, all the different parts of my identity collided. I've spent my whole life feeling like I don't belong. As a queer boy in Islam class, the threat of going to hell because of who I was inside was a very real and perpetual anxiety. Despite being able to leave the Middle East for a liberal Western education that afforded me numerous privileges and opportunities, I faced constant discrimination and prejudice when I won a place at Eton for two years (two of the worst of my life). I've lived between the Middle East and London, and have felt too gay for Iraqis, and too Iraqi for gays. My non-binary gender identity has meant that I don't feel comfortable in most gendered spaces – gay male clubs, for instance – and I regularly feel out of place in my own male body, as though it doesn't match up to who I am internally. For a long time, I felt as if I belonged under water, in a marine world with colours to rival the outfits of any RuPaul drag queen, where things flow freely, formlessly and without judgement, where difference is revealed to be the very fabric of this universe. On land I've felt like a suffocating beached whale, unable to swim to anyone or anywhere.

But that Edinburgh night, as the beautiful girl in the hijab held my hand and reassured me of Allah's unconditional love and I stood in front of her in a sequin leotard and a melting face of sapphire glitter, I finally felt as if I belonged.

The December before that Edinburgh summer, I decided to get a unicorn tattooed across my chest. Christmas is one of the hardest periods for me every year; the months leading up to it are saturated with pictures of united families in green paper crowns beaming around the dinner table, and the dominant cultural narrative tells us that it's the time to be with the real people who know and love us the most. Most friends of mine retreat to the houses they were raised in for cosy, Hallmark-worthy reunions, acquaintances post gifts from partners on Instagram, and it is the time I feel most divorced from Britain, the Middle East, my family, and, well, the world. So to keep me company for the holiday season, I invited a permanent-ink unicorn to live above my sternum.

I feel a great affinity with unicorns. They are the ultimate outsiders, destined to gallop alone. They share the body of a horse and are similar in form, but are of a different nature, almost able to belong in an equine herd, but utterly conspicuous and irrefutably other. For, no matter what, their fantastical horn cannot be concealed, signifying that they are of a different order entirely. In some medieval renderings of unicorns, the horns bring with them the sense of the pathetic; they are a deformity that invites the outside world to taunt the special being, almost like a dunce. As someone who has felt displaced for so long, I've harboured resentment for my own obtrusive horn, which has made it impossible for me to assimilate anywhere.

But as much as the horn is an unwelcome protrusion, perhaps even a social inconvenience, it is also a symbol of pride, of a creature flaunting its difference without shame. For the horn also tells us that the unicorn is a survivor, a rare and tenacious creature, ready to fight should its difference bring it in the way of violence. For me, the multiple meanings of unicorns encapsulate the very essence of being queer. Their identity challenges the status quo and is violated by the normative. They long to gallop in a herd, but struggle to ride to the rhythm of others. They can almost hide in plain sight, and yet are also unquestionably unique.

Like a unicorn, I've never been able to escape my difference from others. As someone who's always existed between cultures, classes, genders, and racial groups, I have what society deems an 'intersectional' identity. The concept of 'intersectionality' refers to the fact that we cannot study the issues surrounding one oppressed social group without understanding its intersections with many others; for instance, it is superficial to have a feminism that dismantles systems of misogyny without also understanding how this intersects with structures of racism (when examining the wage gap for instance, it's critical to consider not only the disparity between men and women, but the one between white women and women of colour). And, though mine is an extreme example of this, every person's identity contains multiple facets that intersect with each other internally, and which are represented by intersecting political and social arguments in the outside world. Sometimes these intersections coexist peacefully; sometimes they are in conflict, and tear us into pieces.

My intersectional identity has never felt stable. The best way I can describe it is to say that it's like playing a really exhausting game of Twister with yourself all day every day, a key part of your identity choke-holding you on one end of the flimsy plastic sheet, while you wrap your legs around its opponent on the other. All the various facets of my identity have pulled each other in polarising directions, leading at times to absurd contradictions, episodes of severe disorientation, and deep internal fractures.

The tattoo artist who gave me my unicorn is a wonderful queer practitioner called Jose Vigers. With an empathetic ear and unreserved generosity of spirit, Jose listened as I explained over Skype what unicorns meant to me. After some wonderfully collaborative discussions, we settled on the design that now armours my heart: a unicorn, being attacked with arrows, on the cusp of collapsing, but strengthened by a BDSM harness and its enduring fighting horn. I wanted a picture that relayed both fragility and strength: an image of a being whose very power and ability to survive derive from the pain they have suffered.

I hope that the story I am about to tell will paint a similar picture.

FEAR AND LOVING IN THE MIDDLE EAST

'Mama, should I get us a condom?' I was eight years old when I asked her this. We were taking our regular joint evening nap. I lay entangled in her embrace – my father, as usual, was travelling with work – and my fingers swam through her silky golden locks, as if their depths were infinite. At that age, my mother had convinced me that eating roast chicken would result in jewel-tinted hair, but I know now that she had what we call 'highlights'.

I had heard the word condom a few times by the age of eight – not in my school's daily Islam lessons, nor at Iftar, the nightly family meal we shared to break our fast during Ramadan, but from the American sitcoms that occasionally sneaked their way through to Bahraini TV networks. I had ascertained that condoms were used between husbands and wives, or boyfriends and girlfriends. Not understanding what sex was, I presumed a condom was a gift shared between people who love each other, only to be bestowed in a bed (it was as a gay adult that I learnt what an apotropaic gift a condom truly was). And so, after a process of logical deduction, I was confident that I fully understood the true definition of condoms.

And here was the perfect opportunity: I was tightly wrapped in the person I loved most on this earth, and in the designated location for this American gifting ritual. I detached myself partially from her maternal clutch, and looked up at her with the earnest expression of a dog expecting a treat for not shitting inside. 'Mama, should I get us a condom?'

My mother's eyes, which I had only ever known to be a source of unending nourishment and affection, changed from their comforting almond shape to a severe angular squint, as if a demon possessed her, an enraged serpent imprisoned behind her glassy pupils. We were gridlocked in this glare of purgatory for what felt like the length of my entire childhood thus far.

'WHERE DID YOU HEAR THAT, AMROU?' The severity of her interrogation caused an unsettling warble in her voice. 'WHY ARE YOU SAYING THIS?' This horrified woman was not one I had ever encountered before, and I felt, for the first time in my life, genuinely scared of her. My strategy was to revert to our tried-and-tested form of interaction, and so I responded with: 'But Mama, it's because I love you.'

My mother leapt up off the bed, my fingers ripped from her halo of golden hair, and she chanted in Arabic, praying to Allah for guidance. If I had known what drag was at the time, I'd probably have enjoyed the melodrama; my mother's white silk dressing gown floated around her as if she were a deity carried by clouds (albeit ones crackling with lightning), and she had all the fiery passion of an Almodóvar heroine. Her thunderous roar eventually subsided as she came to realise that I had no clue what the true function of a condom was, and she sat on the bed in a funerary pose, huddling away from me like someone who had just suffered a Dementor's kiss. I tried to nuzzle my way back into the nest, but as I lay my head on her lap, she brushed me off, and told me to go to my room.

It was at this moment that I had the tragic realisation that the bond between us was not sacred. I became aware of my capacity to transgress; until this point, the idea of anything restricting our love was utterly alien. Something *I* said had revealed boundaries to what I believed was a boundless love. As I lay in my bed that evening – my twin brother Ramy sleeping soundly on the bed next to me – the weight of this overwhelmed me, and I wept so hard that I was eventually exhausted.

How could anything I do upset Mama? Are there things happening in my brain and body that might cause her to reject me? It felt like the purity of our bond was stained for ever. My mother was the light and love of my life, so the idea that there could be something other than love between us filled me with a terror that has endured till this day. In all honesty, I think it governs pretty much everything I do.

Following 'Mama-condom-gate', I made it my immediate mission to repair any fissures between us. My strategies ranged from the sweet and charming to the dangerous and really quite alarming.

The first tactic was to remind my mother how cherubic I was, to eradicate any notion of me as at all transgressive. Mama always lay my and Ramy's pyjamas on our beds following our evening showers – here was the perfect opportunity to intervene. And so, every night for the week that followed, I beat her to this, as a way to dazzle her with the sanctity of my little heart. And I was victorious. When Mama witnessed my act of complete 'selflessness', she was so moved that she cried with joy, and rewarded me with one of my favourite activities – the aeroplane game. This involved Mama lying on the floor and putting her feet up in the air so my tummy could rest on them, allowing me to fly above her while gazing into her mahogany eyes. *RESULT.* But as the week dragged on, the novelty wore off (on her side, anyway), and Mama grew frustrated with the number of creases caused by my unfolding techniques. Mama, you see, was an aesthetic perfectionist – you might even say an aesthetic dictator. My parents' finances were precarious during my early childhood, and so the need to maintain an external image of aesthetic perfection was paramount. Mama has an odd sense of priority; she was more upset when I once wore socks that had holes in them to school than the time I got attacked by a neighbour's *very* toothy dog. And so, when Mama realised that our expensive pyjamas had developed wrinkles, she told me to stop putting out the clothes because I kept getting it wrong. *POOP. Wrong. I'm wrong. Will she ever see me as right again?*

Playing Mama at her own game was a poor tactic – why attempt to do something that she could always do better than me? If 'Mama-condom-gate' had robbed me of my childhood innocence, then I needed to remind her that I was still only a child.

Early one night, I was playing in the pool that we shared with all the houses in our compound. It was a characteristically unremarkable evening. My brother and I were sinking toy ships in the water – probably inspired by the same early-millennium morbidity that led to the murder of millions of Sims on PCs – and our new nanny was supervising us nearby, so relaxed in the autumn Bahrani heat that she was snoring. Knowing that my mother would be arriving home at any second, I decided to scream for her. I can't with clarity remember my precise thought process, but something about the embryonic feeling of being submerged in water stimulated my idea. I knew what I had to do. And so I screamed 'Mama!' at the top of my lungs, over and over and over again. My brother watched me, totally bemused, and soon enough, behind the corrugated-iron fence surrounding the pool, I saw the legs of my mother, restricted by the mauve pencil skirt she wore to the hospital where she worked as a translator, sprinting towards the gate, until she burst through, panting in front of me with the frail regality of a Hitchcock victim. When my mother saw me treading water, smiling widely because she was home from work, she slumped onto a deckchair and bundled me up, kissing me all over my face, even though I was soaking wet.

Later that evening, I went to find Mama in her bedroom, hoping to rekindle the lost innocence of our evening nap, but she was in a deep sleep. The mascara stains down her face told me she had been crying. When our nanny saw that I had sneaked myself in, she escorted me out, explaining that my mother needed to rest. 'You made her think you were drowning earlier, Amrou. She was terrified. You need to let her rest now.'

And so for the second time that week, I stayed up all night and cried in a frenzy of self-loathing. I was certain I hadn't intended my mother to think I was on the edge of death – *or did I? Am I that cruel? No, I'm just a kid!* But I *had* engineered a scenario that would result in her running to me. *I was just excited to see her, that's all. I miss Mama all the time.*

In the weeks that followed, I interpreted any evasiveness from my mother as her thinking I was fucked-up for my poolside act of emotional manipulation. She felt further away from me than ever, and I yearned for a time before my purity was called into question. One evening after school, a day during which I ached to be reunited with her, Mama spent hours gossiping with friends on the phone. I watched her as she glided around the kitchen, delicately holding out a Marlboro Red cigarette. I was so envious of her friends on the end of the line, who had the privilege of being audience to Mama's hilarious anecdotes. A few times during the evening, I wrapped my arms around her torso as she stayed glued to the phone. With that anthropologically curious way you can let someone know to stop touching you by squeezing them with a firm, conclusive gesture, Mama fetched a baklava from the counter, put it in my mouth, and definitively detached me. In the living room next door, my brother and father were watching football together – an activity so profoundly unenticing to me that the sheer boredom of it could lead me into an existential 'what is the point of life?' spiral, even as a toddler – and so my desire for maternal communion only intensified.

As I went back into the kitchen, where Mama now sipped a Turkish coffee as she laughed infectiously on the phone, I asked her when she would be done – at which she shooed me off, loath to interrupt the flow of what was clearly a banging anecdote. *Those lucky women on the other line!* The situation was desperate. Mama was slipping away from me, and she urgently needed to remember what we had. My eyes darted around the kitchen, searching for a remedy. *Maybe I could spill water on the floor and pretend to slip?* My not being a stuntman threw this one off the drawing board. *Maybe I could pretend to break a vase?* My mother had a passion for expensive tropical flowers – or maybe just things that were expensive, period – so I decided this would do more damage than good. And then I spotted the steaming bronze Turkish coffee pot on the cooker, the shimmer of its Arabesque metallic belly beckoning me towards it. Like a cunning magpie, I made a beeline, and picked it up with my bare hands, incinerating my right palm until I screamed in agony. When Mama saw what had happened, she dropped the phone, grabbed my hand and put it under cold running water as I sobbed into her arms. She was mine again.

She was mine for the rest of the night. Because my hand was so badly blistered from the 'accident', she stayed with me as I slept. I lay on the couch, with her on the floor next to me, holding up my hand so that I didn't hurt it during my sleep. And she sat like this until I woke up the next morning – my beautiful, generous mother. Now I realise these were extreme measures to take for a moment of maternal comfort. But believe me when I tell you: there was no other option besides Mama.

Dubai was my home until the age of seven, Bahrain till I was eleven. Where I was raised, there was a marked distinction between the masculine and the feminine. I grew accustomed to binaries from a very early age, even though I had no awareness of the concept of them. The earliest recollection I have of a strict division between the sexes was when my mother drove to the border of Saudi Arabia (my brother and I were curious to see it). My mother edged to the border and drove away again. 'But Mama, we want to go in,' I implored, confused about what was stopping her. 'Women aren't allowed to drive in Saudi,' my mother said with a remarkable calm, as if the patriarchy lived harmoniously inside her, at one with her brain and mouth. 'Oh, OK,' I said, mirroring my mother's breezy tone. But this was only one incident among many that erected a strict scaffolding of gender rules inside me. Gender segregation was so embedded into the fabric of life that it was impossible not to internalise it and believe it was utterly normal. In mosques, men and women prayed in separate areas; in many Muslim countries, even the form and methods of prayer change depending on your gender. And when it comes to secular activities, the Middle East can be remarkably homosocial (you could say ironically so).

Like schoolchildren separated into queues of girls and boys before PE, my parents always split up when entertaining guests at home. My mother drank tea and smoked with the other wives in one room – all of them trampling over each other to show off the most recent designer pieces, as though it was some label-obsessed *Lord of the Flies* – while my dad and the husbands claimed the larger room, where they puffed on cigars and gambled. When my brother and I were 'lucky', we were invited to the pews of masculinity, giving us an insight into the cunning rules of poker – 'lying to make money' I called it – and tuning our ears to conversations about business (also lying to make money). Ramy clearly felt privileged to have access to this space, and wherever possible would initiate poker games with his own friends in a classic case of social reproduction, all of them future Arab homeboys in the making.

One night, when the whisky-scented card game was drawing to a close, I excused myself to go to bed. As I made my way, I hovered by the corner of the women's quarter, peering in to get a glimpse of a world with which my heart felt more aligned. This was a room to which I needed the key; each guest was decked in enough jewellery to make the collective room feel like a vault at Gringotts (*yes*, I like Harry Potter), and textured fabrics of the richest emerald, sapphire, and ruby hues. The conversational mannerisms were dynamic and poetic. I watched with wonder as my mother entertained her guests, how she conducted their laughter as if the room were an orchestral pit, channelling an energy diametrically opposed to the square masculinity next door.

My mother's Middle East was the one I felt safe in; this was especially the case the more Islam dominated my life. As a child, I was taught to be extremely God-fearing, and Allah, in my head, was a paternalistic punisher. He could have been another man at the poker table, but one much mightier, more severe than the ones I knew, one who might put his cigar out on my little head.

22

From as early as I can remember, I was forced to attend Islam class every week at school. When I got to Bahrain, the lessons went from warm and fuzzy – where Allah was a source of unending generosity and love – to terrifying, forcing open a Pandora's box I'll never be able to close completely.

At each lesson, the other children and I sat jittery at our desks and looked up at the Islam teacher. Her ethereal Arab robes cloaked stern arthritic hands and the billowing black fabric affirmed her piety. Her warnings about Allah's punishments were grave. We were taught that throughout our lives, any sin committed would invite a disappointed angel to place bad points on our left shoulder, while any good deeds would allow an angel to place rewarding points on our right. Sins were remarkably easy to incur, and could stem from the most natural of thoughts – *I'm jealous of that girl's fuchsia pencil case* – while good deeds were nearly impossible to achieve at such a young age, and only counted when you made an active, positive change in the world, like significantly helping a homeless person (a hard task for any seven-year-old). Sins, Islamic class taught us, hovered everywhere around us, and we had to do whatever possible to avoid them. Any time a slipper or a shoe faced its bottom up to the sky – an unimaginable insult to Allah – we'd be hit with a wad of negative points (it's important to note that many things we know to be sins were inherited from cultural traditions rather than the Quran). And so, once I moved to Bahrain, I developed a compulsive habit of scanning any room I entered for upside-down footwear; I'd sprint around houses like a crazed plate-spinner, burdening myself with endless bad points for having got to each piece of footwear too late. These upside-down shoes would cost me up to fifty sins a day, each one a hit of fiery ash from the cigar above my head. Till this day, in fact, I still turn over any upside-down slipper or shoe that I find. And as a young child, I felt so desperate for these elusive positive points on my right shoulder, that at one point I decided I would be a policeman when I grew up, so as to make a career out of acquiring good deeds (little did I know of institutional police corruption).

The consequences of a heavier left shoulder were gravely impressed upon us. In short – as a sinner, you were *fucked*. Each week in class, we were made to close our eyes and imagine ourselves in the following situation: an earthquake tearing open the earth on its final day, forcing all corpses to crawl out of their graves and travel to purgatory for Judgement Day. Here, Allah would weigh our points in front of everyone we knew, who would come to learn all our sinful thoughts about them. And of course, if one incurred more sins than good deeds during one's life, the only result was an eternity of damnation in Satan's lair. As in any gay fetish club worth your money, the activities on offer include: lashing, being bound in rope, and humiliation – except none of it is consensual, it never stops, and you're also being scalded with fire the whole time. Twenty years since being taught these torturous visual exercises, I am still subject to a recurring nightmare where Allah himself has pinned me to a metal torture bed surrounded by fire, and incinerates my body as he interrogates me for all my transgressions. Around twice a week, this nightmare wakes me up to a bed pooled in sweat (and, weirdly, once in a while, cum).

My left shoulder quickly outweighed my right in points. Of course there were the everyday misdeeds – *my brother is annoying me, this food is dry, I think my cousin smells* – that occupied my sin-charting angel, like a passive-aggressive driving instructor totting up minor faults. But there were also the major indictments. For instance, at the age of nine, as I was daydreaming in a lesson, I unthinkingly drew the outline of a bum on the Quran – thereby committing the ultimate defacement and simultaneously betraying an unconscious association between anal sex and religion that's probably straight out of the psychoanalysis textbook. This blasphemy was a crime of such gravity that there was an entire school inquisition, with all the kids in my year group forced to produce writing samples. There I was, sitting on the sizzling hot concrete outside the headmaster's office, trying to figure out how many good deeds I'd need to settle the insurmountable difference, yet also plotting to botch the test to get another child in trouble.

I got off the hook. After my writing sample was checked, I was told I could go home. On the bus back from school, I remember staring at the sandy pavements, and being struck by how many heavy rocks and boulders there were lying around all over the streets. I counted each one I could see, feeling the weight of every stone in my conscience, all colliding together to create an avalanche of heavy guilt, knowing that some poor Muslim child was getting the punishment of their life for defacing the Quran with an arse.

This obsessive sin collecting had developed into a pretty debilitating OCD by the time I was ten. Here's how it manifested. Since doctors were highly respected by my family and community – particularly male doctors – I told my parents I wanted to be one, and asked them to enrol me in an after-school first-aid club (and you thought Glee Club was as lame as it gets?). It was here that I learnt of an acronym that ensnared my brain – DR. ABC. It's short for **Danger, Response, Airway, Breathing, Circulation**, and it's the order of things to assess when you see someone in peril. You look around to evaluate the threat of surrounding **Danger**. You make noise and prod to see if the victim in question **Responds**. You ascertain whether their **Airway** is clear. You check to see if they're **Breathing**. And you search for a pulse to feel for any **Circulation**. **DR. ABC**. It was the key to saving life. DR. ABC. It was the key to doing good. While the exhausted angel on my left shoulder forever beavered away, turning every single moment in time into a concoction of misdemeanours, I had DR. ABC at the forefront of my consciousness, driving me towards the light. Let me explain.

In the first stages, I muttered DR. ABC under my breath at any chance I could. Obsessively repeating DR. ABC meant I wouldn't have the mental capacity to commit a sin. While my left shoulder was sinking under its wealth of sin, DR. ABC was like a lifeguard, rescuing me from a tarry ocean of transgressions. Let's say I was sitting at home, with my brother and father yelping while the football played on TV; my DR. ABC incantation would stop any sinful, negative thoughts from forming, such as hoping the TV exploded. During Islamic Ramadan, a month during which we fasted all day as a demonstration of our piety, any internal dubiousness I had over Allah's rationale to starve his people was diverted by DR. ABC. When my subconscious felt like I was plummeting down a sharp steep cliff edge, DR. ABC was a bit of rope to hang on to, slowing down the inevitable descent. DR. ABC became my form of control. But then, like all systems implementing order, it started to control me. And eventually, it enslaved me.

In periods where I felt especially rotten inside, it would come out with a vengeance. For instance, if I was having a bad day and someone spoke to me, I would count the number of syllables they used through the acronym DR. ABC. So let's say a classmate at school said, 'Amrou, do you have a spare rubber?' That's nine syllables. And so, in my head I would mutter DR. ABC until I reached nine syllables – D. R. A. B. C. D. R. A. B. Ending on *B*, my eraser-depleted classmate would now be characterised as a *B* in my mind. Then imagine the teacher chimed in: 'Amrou, hand in your homework.' Seven syllables, D. R. A. B. C. D. R. – *R*. So they became an *R*. And on and on this would go, exhaustingly charting the letter-position of everyone who spoke, balancing the syllable counts of the room like a juggler on crack, all to uphold the fascistic order of DR. ABC.

DR. ABC, my new male oppressor, was always buzzing about, calmed only by being with Mama.

As Allah and DR. ABC enacted a mental tug of war with a masculine brutishness, Mama offered a mystical feminine grace of a different order entirely. While public expectation called for a strict separation of the genders, the rules seemed to fall apart for us in private.

I think this was particularly due to the peculiar set-up of our family unit; for the most part, my brother was raised by my father, and I was raised by my mother. (This is why Ramy doesn't play much of a part in this book – well, until right at the end, when he steps in and has a very significant role.) Weekends were centred around what Ramy and I wanted to do. Ramy enjoyed playing football and going to the arcade; my father was passionate about football, and enjoyed the camaraderie this gave him with Ramy. Baba was also usually drained from his long weeks at work, and enjoyed any activity that required no emotional commit-ment. My favourite pastime was going to the mall with

Mama, and I spent most weekends watching her try on clothes and get her hair blow-dried at the salon (how I loved observing her gossip with the hairdressers, marvelling at the waves of her rich Arab hair and hearing the chorus of laughter that greeted her anecdotes). Whenever Mama was driving, I always seemed to be in the front seat of her car; Ramy was Baba's passenger. Among relatives, it became a family mythology that Amrou was Mama's and Ramy Baba's; in all honesty, it sometimes feels like we had separate childhoods with little overlap.

'Amoura,' Mama sang from her bedroom one evening, a tune that I was more than happy to follow. For I knew what this musical tone meant. 'Yes, Mama?' I said with a performed coyness, knowing full well the treat that awaited me. Mama was going out to dinner with friends, and she needed help deciding which pair of shoes to wear. Her left foot flaunted a short-heeled, patent silver, open-toe number – *divine* – while her right foot donned a more sensible boot, though not without its embellishments, which included studs, and gold eyelets for the laces. Like a runway model posing for a designer, Mama switched from profile to profile so I could assess the full picture before giving my vote. I went for the silver (a total no-brainer). My mother winked at me, then fetched a baklava sweet from her make-up table, which she fed me as she stroked my hair, chanting, 'My clever boy. My clever, darling boy.' Mama and I knew that she was going to choose the silver shoe all along, but this performance was all part of our secret language. She knew I was illiterate in football, but the grammar of glamorous footwear – in this I was fluent.

There were other iterations of our secret club. When my brother and father went to play in the park, I would stay in to 'finish my homework'. Once the echoes of football studs against the marble floor were no more, I emerged from my bedroom to be with Mama. This usually entailed me sitting with her on the couch as she painted her nails, smoked her cigarettes, and gossiped on the phone to a background of whatever the Egyptian networks were airing on our TV. It was during one of these sensory sofa experiences that I witnessed the magic of Umm Kulthum.

As Mama was flicking through the channels, a powerful voice flowed out of the TV screen. The moment this happened, Mama put down the phone, and both our heads turned simultaneously. This sonorous voice had the depth and gravitas of a gargantuan black hole that nothing would escape. The vibrato of her chords felt more like a tremor, as if each note was sending the room into a seismic shock that grabbed your insides until you were crying without realising. And not only was her voice able to take up – even alter – space, but her presence was of a might that I'd only ever associated before with the force of Allah. A large woman, she stood rooted to the spot onstage, her hair towering above her in a perfectly constructed up-do, her ears enveloped by enormous oval diamonds, and as she sang each heartbreaking note, she wrung her hands together with all the intensity of a grieving mother.

'Mama … who is that?' I said. My voice came out whispering and faint, as though Umm Kulthum had sucked in its power to strengthen her own.

'Hayatti ('my life'), that's Umm Kulthum: she was the most famous singer in the world.'

Mama explained how Umm Kulthum (1898–1975) – oddly, her name translates as 'mother of the male elephant' – was an Egyptian singer who had taken the Arab world by storm. She was the most notorious singer of her time, known for a voice so powerful that it would break microphones if she stood too close to them. 'You see how far away the microphone is on the stage? That's so it doesn't break.' Her performance on TV was transcendentally majestic, and the response of her audience would make a Gaga concert look like an episode of *Countdown*. I watched with fascination as grown Arab men, dressed in traditional Islamic gear, broke their patriarchal stoicism and wept in front of their wives, who themselves stood up and ululated at Umm Kulthum. This feminine deity had the power to crumble the strict gendered behavioural rules that governed our communities. A fuzzy, comforting feeling started to circulate in my bloodstream. Hope.

And so I lay my head on Mama's silky lap, as her indigo-manicured hands brushed my hair with the delicacy of a feather. But as I closed my eyes, the velvety bass timbre of Umm Kulthum's voice gradually became the shadowy echo of an Islamic call to prayer. The shift in mood woke me from my hypnagogic dozing, and I realised that it was the male voice of an Imam interrupting the TV broadcast, as happened five times a day on Muslim networks. I fell asleep with ease that night, thinking that even though I had missed my prayer that evening, my sofa time with both the elephant's mother and my own was its own kind of religious experience.

Umm Kulthum was a matriarchal version of the Middle East I wished I knew more of. During Islam lessons, as our teachers reminded us of our inevitable damnation, I would close my eyes and think of Umm Kulthum, the true ruler of Arabia.

Part of Islam class involved learning verses in the Quran – surahs – off by heart, so that we could recite them during prayer. The importance of our knowing these by memory was impressed upon us with severity; we could be called at random to recite a surah in front of the class, and detention awaited us if we weren't able to. I've had the fortune of a photographic memory my whole life, so was always able to have these surahs down. And learning an Umm Kulthum song was not dissimilar to learning an Islamic surah. Umm Kulthum's songs were similar in form to Islamic prayer – they felt more like incantations with no fixed melody, were often thirty minutes long, and the concerts they resulted in were practically spaces of worship.

I asked my mother to buy me some Umm Kulthum CDs to play in my Discman – remember how even the slightest movement would jolt the music in those? – and her voice would hypnotise me until I fell asleep. Umm Kulthum chanting in my ear was an anaesthetic against DR. ABC, as if all the water in the River Nile ran through me, calming every one of my demons with its soporific embrace. And after my week with Umm Kulthum (the coming-of-age Arab sequel to Simon Curtis's *My Week with Marilyn*?) I had learnt one of her fifteen-minute songs off by heart. When my father was away with work one week, I woke my mother up in the middle of the night and sang it to her note by note. With a smile that could thaw even Putin's cold, dead heart, she watched my solo performance, and invited me back into bed with her once I had finished the song. This time, I was sure not to suggest we find ourselves a condom.

Holding onto Mama was the only way I could feel safe in a culture and faith that was really starting to scare me. The idea that we might ever be separated was a thought too horrifying to entertain, and I had to do whatever possible to keep her close. This took quite a literal turn when I became obsessed with grabbing my mother's thighs. Whenever Mama and I were separated for longer than I was used to – if, say, it was my father whose car I was in for the weekend, or if she was late from work, and Islam class had been particularly terrifying that day – one of the first things I would do was beg to play with her thighs; more specifically, the bit that jiggled on the inside of her legs. This might sound slightly sordid, but I assure you it was completely innocent and utterly calming. When Mama emerged from her bedroom in one of her airy silk dressing gowns, she would sit on the couch to watch TV and smoke, allowing me, if no one else was there, to shake the loose bit of muscle on the inside of her thigh. I found its soft, buoyant texture deeply calming, as if her flesh were like a stress ball that could assuage any anxieties about my status as a sinner. Enveloping myself in her flesh was like burying my face in a silk pillow, a site of utter relaxation and peace from the terrors of the world outside. This activity was such a habitual remedy that when Mama could sense I was having a particularly bad day, she would open up her dressing gown and present her leg to me, the calming cushion to all my fears.

My father was clearly insecure about the unashamed preference I had for Mama, so one evening he took Ramy and me out to dinner for 'a boys' night'. I dreaded the evening to my core. Not because I didn't want to be with them, but because I didn't want to be apart from Mama. To be honest, I can't remember much of the evening, except one quite alarming moment. As I excused myself to go to the toilet for the eighth time during the main course, I glimpsed the back of Mama's head at a table in the smoking section of the restaurant (a smoking section – how vintage!). I felt suddenly elated that my time in the boys' corner might be over sooner than I expected. I sprinted over to her and wrapped my arms around her neck as if we were two conjoined swans, burrowing myself into her hair. She jumped up in shock and turned around, severing me from her embrace as she did so. When I looked up at her

… she was not my mother. She was just another Arab woman of my mother's age (who potentially used the same hairdresser). I apologised, and drooped back to Baba and Ramy, embarrassed and upset. All I wanted was to be with Mama. I was *all* about my mother.

When it was just me and Mama, we created a pocket of 'camp' that only we were privy too. And it was in this special fortress that my love of performance was born. Now, Dubai and Bahrain had no culture of theatre – literally, *none* – and so my only access was a VHS tape of *CATS* on the West End that I received as a gift from some cousins in London. Until I was a teenager, I thought *CATS* was the pinnacle of Britain's rich theatrical history. In truth, I believed that it was the only *real* bit of theatre that mattered. The first time I watched it, I was struck by the way male bodies were celebrated for their balletic curves, how they flaunted chic feline poses with utter pride, sitting side by side with the female performers without any shame. Now, my homosexual desires hadn't quite taken shape when I was nine, and sexual desire was not a concept anyone articulated (in fact, one of my Muslim cousins only learnt that pregnancy was the result of sex, rather than marriage, at the age of sixteen); but the way that the musculature of the male performers was embellished by their spandex costumes sparked a feeling in me that had been lying dormant until that moment. *All I have to do is get to*

London, and then I'll be able to roll around with the span-dex male cats. This became a definitive, serious ambition of mine, and I told my mother that I wanted to be a performer so that I could be in *CATS* in the West End one day.

Because Bahrain was so bereft of theatre, Mama turned into Miss Marple in her quest to find me a stage – no doubt my midnight impersonation of Umm Kulthum had convinced her of my chops. Her investigative efforts led her to discover that the British Council often held a Christmas pantomime as a way to preserve the cultural tradition. She called them up and explained that her young son was desperate for a part – but they said this was more a produc-tion for British citizens living in the Middle East. My brother and I had British passports; when we were yet unborn in our mother's tummy, she and my dad had left Saddam Hussein's regime in Iraq and we were born in Camden, thus granting us immediate British citizenship (Theresa May wasn't in the Home Office yet). But then they told Mama that there were no roles for children in the pantomime. Undeterred, with the might of Umm Kulthum, and the tenacity of Erin Brockovich, Mama marched me into the British Council building the next day, and demanded they give me a part. But in this amateur produc-tion of *Cinderella*, there just *wasn't* a part for a child. And so we were forced to drive home, tears running down my face, in a melodramatic tableau I wish had been filmed for posterity.

The next evening, as I mourned my non-existent panto-mime career on the sofa in front of the TV, Mama came running from the kitchen, excitement all over her face as if she'd just won the lottery. 'Amoura! Pick up the house phone – there's someone on the line.' *Was it Baba, wanting to know if I'd join him and Ramy at the kebab shop for the umpteenth time?* I had an excuse pursed on my lips, but I was caught completely by surprise – it was the director of the pantomime! He said he was so impressed with my determination to have a role in his production, that he had written one into the script for me – yes, you heard me: a role created specially for *me*.

To my knowledge, this character existed in no version of *Cinderella* throughout history, but I was ecstatic nonethe-less. For I was going to be premiering the never-before-seen role of … the Fairy Godmother's *gecko*. You heard it. A gecko. In *Cinderella*. My first foray into show business was to play a GECKO in a story that had nothing to do with geckos. Who knows, maybe the casting of a brown boy as an exotic reptile was rooted in systemic colonial structures – this was the British Council after all – but at the time, I felt nothing but victorious.

Rehearsals were after school every evening. I was the only child in the production, and because the gecko was – surprise! – not exactly integral to the plot, I really wasn't needed much. However, I told Mama that I needed to be at every single rehearsal if I was going to do the part any justice. *What is the world this gecko is inhabiting? Is this gecko scared of the Ugly Sisters too? Has the gecko been watching Cinderella's abuse their whole life?* – there were many urgent things to interrogate. In reality, all I had to do was stand in front of Cinderella as she got changed from rags to riches in the ball sequence. Effectively, I was a shield – a role so perfunctory that at the last minute they roped in my twin brother so that he could provide extra block-age. Despite my role as a wall divide, Mama sat with me in every single rehearsal as I soaked up the colourful world of pantomime and its diverse cast of performers.

Remember how, as a kid, a lot of your time was spent looking up at adults with a fiery curiosity? Remember how BIG every grown-up seemed? How each grown-up was like a speculative mirror to your future self, and you imagined yourself living the incredible lives you presumed they had? And there were some grown-ups who seemed different to any other grown-up you'd seen before – who took on a prophetic status, as if your paths crossing was an act of divine intervention? There were two such adults in the pantomime – and they were the grown men playing the Ugly Sisters. Both were from England, in their late thirties/ early forties, and with hindsight I think they were a couple, but at the time I believed them to be best friends. From my minuscule height they seemed to have imposing, manly frames, yet they gestured with their hands as if they were flicking wands, oozing wit and comic flare – what we might term 'camp'. 'Were you in *CATS*?' I asked them one evening with complete sincerity, at which they laughed from the belly, one of them commenting: 'Darling, I *wish.*' Yes, I *wish too. We get each other.*

During one dress rehearsal, I was completely blown away when both men came onto the stage in women's clothing. I remember their costumes vividly; one of them had bright orange pigtails, radio-active fuchsia lips, and freckles dotted all over his face, while the other had a plum-toned up-do of a shape not dissimilar to Umm Kulthum's. The former had what looked like a pink chequered apron flowing down his body, while the other was strapped into a purple corset and black thigh-high boots. With little conception of my gender or sexuality at this point, I can't remember processing my own dysphoria or sexual orientation within what I was seeing – the overarching feeling I had was, 'is this allowed?' I looked around the room, seeing the rest of the cast laugh and celebrate both men in their feminine get-ups. The pair were melding the masculine and the feminine, transgressing both, relishing both, and there was nothing dangerous about it – all it brought into the room was a feeling of collective joy. Just as Umm Kulthum's voice could apparently overcome audience gender divides, again I was witnessing the potential of femininity to alter social space. Rules and codes of behavioural conduct formed a major part of Islamic teachings, so the idea of a man transgressing his gender codes was not something I thought I'd ever see publicly in the Middle East. But here, in front of me, were men wearing women's clothing, and the only reactions they provoked were ones of enjoyment. I was smiling goofily, and, as I turned to my mother, I could see that she too was enjoying the performance of the two infectious, loveable queens. *Mama's enjoying this too! Maybe not being a manly boy will be OK with Mama!* It seemed that in our secret club, these other ways of being were tolerated – celebrated, even. Perhaps I had nothing to worry about.

But, as I would shortly learn, Mama's and my bubble was going to burst. And in the next phase of my life, nothing could have prepared me for how sharp a turn Mama would take to stop me being different.

The first proper realisation I had of being gay was at the age of ten. I was at home watching TV when the cartoon of *Robin Hood* aired. And let me tell you: I crushed *hard* on Mr Hood (the cartoon fox, not the actual historical figure). Now I promise you I'm not into bestiality, but the arousal I experienced was an extension of the titillation I had felt for the men wearing spandex in *CATS*, only this time it was tangibly sexual. The cartoon character wore a remarkably progressive gender-queer T-shirt, which was long enough to cover his groin, but he wore it with no bottoms, and cinched at the waist with a River-Island type belt. The way the garment billowed around the character's pelvis had me fixated, and I was desperate to know what lay underneath – to be frank, I was hungry for a bite of it (minus the fur, but definitely *with* the balls). His stud status was accentuated by muscular thighs and an ability to penetrate enemies with his bow and arrow, and, as I watched, I imagined myself by his side, a little damsel in distress who he would make it his mission to protect.

I knew that it wouldn't be the best idea to verbalise my crush to anyone – but I needed to investigate my desires more closely. So when the whole house was asleep one night, I locked myself in the bathroom, got naked, and lay on the marble floor, imagining Robin Hood – yes, the cartoon fox – next to me. The texture of the cold floor against my sweaty torso created a tingling sensation, and the pitch-black midnight of the room made for a psycho-sensory experience. Pretty quickly, it felt like Mr Hood was next to me, and I started writhing around the floor, my aroused body fusing with the galactic space around me, as if the desire in my body poured through my skin and into Mr. Hood's soul, which was totally consuming me. As the experience intensified, the more out-of-body it became, and I lost all sense of my physicality, floating in a foamy limbo of ecstasy, as if every atom of my being were being engulfed. The next thing I knew it was 7 a.m., and someone was knocking on the door. It was time for school.

It wasn't long before we were warned about the perils of homosexuality at school. As a Muslim, you were already in a committed, non-negotiable relationship with Allah; the rules, according to our teacher, were that you could open this relationship if it was with a devout Muslim of the opposite gender. A Muslim man dating a non-Muslim woman? Eternal damnation. A Muslim man dating a *man*, period? Eternal damnation ad infinitum. The closer we got to puberty, the more insight we were given into what actually went down in hell. And it was in these lessons that feelings of terror and shame attached themselves like a bloodthirsty parasite to my sexuality.

It is worth noting that it's not entirely clear whether the Quran actually condemns homosexuality. The only passages in which it seems to, in *The Story of Lot*, are ambiguous. In the story, Allah punishes the men of a city for their indecent sexual activities with male visitors. Yet it is not the homosexual act that is being denounced, but rather that the visitors were being raped. It is the way such Quranic passages have been interpreted by conservative Islamic scholars and lawmakers that has partly led to such institutional homophobia among Muslims.

So as I've explained, whether we ended up in hell depended on the points between our left and right shoulders – if those on the left exceeded those on the right, then hell it was:

But he whose balance [of good deeds] is found to be light, will have his home in a [bottomless] Pit. And what will explain to you what this is? A Fire blazing fiercely! (101:8–11)

Cute, right? The snag for me was that I was taught that homosexuality resulted in an automatic infinite number of sins, and no kind of good deed – not even curing cancer or solving climate change – could help compensate. *But I only have a crush on Robin Hood THE FOX – the Quran doesn't say anything about fancying foxes?* I clutched onto this minuscule loophole of hope – I had to. For the punishments of hell were described to us with intimate detail. While water in heaven was a redemptive, cleansing element, in hell we'd be forced to drink and bathe in boiling water. 'Close your eyes and imagine the heat on your skin and in your stomach,' our teacher would tell us. With my eyes shut, I clung onto the lifebuoy that was DR. ABC – but it was no longer enough to stop my whole body from boiling. Another fabulous little treat in store for us was The Tree of Zaqqum, a deceptive piece of foliage whose fruit we'd be forced to eat. When I say 'fruit', I mean little devil heads disguised as fruit, which would mutilate our insides once ingested. And what to drink to wash off the horrific taste? Boiling water, of course. *DR. ABC – what's your cure for a shredded, incinerated gut? Nothing.*

The intensity of hell's punishments had a domino effect that debilitated DR. ABC's capacity to hold off the terror, spreading around my brain like a wildfire that just couldn't be controlled. And then came the final blow in our classroom tour of Satan's lair: the overarching punishment of hell would be our regret that we hadn't changed our behaviour on earth – that we lost Allah – coupled with the knowledge that nothing would placate Allah's rage. We were stuck here for eternity, and it was entirely our fault.

Eternal self-blame was Allah's ultimate punishment, and it's a feeling that has seeped into absolutely everything I experience.

To this day, every single time a traffic light goes red, I experience a pang of anxiety because I fear I've incited its fury. I've tried and tried to shirk this, but it is so engrained into my neurological make-up that I just can't. Another road phenomenon that overwhelms me with guilt is when I press the 'wait' button before crossing a road; if there are no cars coming, I might decide to cross, but sometimes the traffic light then goes red, forcing a car to stop even though I've already crossed the road. I usually feel so bad when this happens that I have to mouth an 'I'm sorry' to the delayed driver every time. And, throughout my life, whenever I've had major doubts about Islam, one of the key thoughts that dissuades me from my scepticism is this: *but just in case Allah is real, I should probably stay Muslim to avoid the not-so-glam time in Lucifer's dungeon.* This shadowy doubt, which I managed to stave off through times with my mother as a kid, became an all-consuming plague when I went from fancying cartoon foxes to actual boys.

The first boy I crushed on was none other than Macaulay Culkin in *Home Alone* – can you honestly tell me *you* didn't when you were a kid? I was ten years old. I knew I was gay by this point. I wanted to cuddle Macaulay Culkin in bed, and had the intense urge to help him through his lonely sorrow in the film. I wanted to support him, to be his partner, to lie naked with him and to feel supported by him. Perhaps it was also because I was starting to feel lonely in the Middle East, and I thought that he and I had a lot in common. When I realised the intensity of my desire, I was terrified by the religious implications of it. What I really wanted to do was cuddle up to Mama and have her and Umm Kulthum sing me to sleep, telling me it was going to be OK; but the fear was all-consuming, and it had to come out of me, for the thought was munching at my insides like a flesh-eating virus. And so I came out with it when we were on a family vacation in London.

Let me set the scene: we were visiting my dad's old childhood friend who worked in the UK (let's call him Majid); unlike most Arab men his age I'd met, he had never been married, and was dating a raucous and infectiously free-spirited English woman (let's call her Lily). They were the first 'interracial' couple I'd ever seen, and much like the panto dames fusing genders, this relationship seemed to bridge cultures, a further sign that there were other models of behaviour outside of what I'd grown up with. Lily had a gay friend (let's call him Billy) who was a fleeting but powerful presence. With bright red hair and toned arms, Billy wore tank tops and denim hot pants, and spoke with a melodic Liverpudlian accent that made every room he was in feel like a scene in an uplifting musical. My interactions with him were slight; when he came over to

Majid's house in Islington, I stayed quiet and read my Jacqueline Wilson 'teenage-girl' books in the corner (they were my favourite), attempting a surreptitious peep over the pages every now and then. I'd never seen a man so effeminate owning space like he did, and as he and the adults – my parents included – chatted over dinner and drinks, he splayed his lean legs over a spare chair, recalibrating the entire rhythm of the room to his own pace. Billy was the mistress of ceremonies in this house now. Lily referred to Billy with a 'she' pronoun throughout the night, and this flexible attitude towards gender seemed entirely accepted, just as it had been with the dames in pantomime. *Perhaps this is only OK in London (or the British Council)?* When I looked at my mother, she also seemed to hang on Billy's every word, and she laughed from the belly in a way that told me she was genuinely delighted by his company. The next day, they even went clothes shopping together, for crying out loud.

The way in which Billy was accepted by everyone – particularly Mama – gave me the confidence that confessing my love for Macaulay Culkin might even be celebrated, despite what I knew about homosexuality from Islam. So as I was having lunch with Majid at a restaurant one afternoon, I said 'I'm in love with Macaulay Culkin.' Majid, who was sipping a whisky and Coca Cola, slowly put down the tumbler.

'Oh yeah,' he said nonchalantly. 'You love him in the film? Because he's a good actor?'

'No! I'm in love with him. I want to marry him.'

Majid picked up his drink and took a big gulp, then he told me to finish my food. His thick eyebrows furrowed as he watched me slurp my spaghetti. The silence was a bit unnerving, but I interpreted his gaze as somewhat benevolent – *maybe he feels the same because he also fancies a white person?* As I found out later that evening, that was definitely not what he was feeling.

As I thumbed a new Jacqueline Wilson book in the guest room that evening, Majid called my name from the living room downstairs. I presumed dinner was ready. But after descending the staircase, I entered a room that was eerily quiet. The TV was off, no food was laid out on the tables, and Majid, my father, and mother were sitting neatly on the living-room couch, like Olympic gymnastics judges, ordered and unreadable. On the sofa next to them sat my brother, Majid's fifteen-year-old son and marijuana-enthusiast, and Lily, who had her eyes glued to the floor. Majid then spoke: 'Is everyone OK if we go out for dinner tonight? There's a tasty Lebanese place near us.' *Phew. This is just a menu meeting.* General mutters of agreement spread around the room. 'But before we go … Amrou, do you want to tell everyone what you told me today?' Mama sat up straight, the fact that I might have confided something to Majid without telling her first clearly upsetting to her. Mama and I didn't keep secrets from each other. But on a cultural level, the fact that I said something to a family friend without first checking it with my parents was also very taboo; where we're from, family units are more like clans. You are less an individual, and more one puzzle-piece of the collective familial-self, where everything that you say or do reflects the entirety of the family tribe. If any member of the family unit displays individual ways of thinking and behaving, the entire clan must come together to control, exile or destroy the offender.

'I don't know what you mean,' I said. My mother's eyes were giving out a hot glare, as if thin infrared lasers were beaming out and trying to penetrate my subconscious.

'About Macaulay Culkin?' *Holy Shitting Fucking Christ on his Fucking Crucifix.*

I looked around the room and assessed the perilous situation. *Maybe I should just tell everyone I'm in love with Macaulay Culkin? I mean, we are in London – the home of spandex male cats, the place where pantomime was born – and look at Lily! She parties in St Tropez and wears revealing clothes – and she's white and dating an Arab! – and WAIT A SECOND, what about Billy, the gay super-hero who my mother LOVES?! Maybe it won't be so bad? What if Islam doesn't exist in this part of North London? OK – I'm going to go for it. What could possibly go wrong?!*

'I told Majid that I'm in love with Macaulay Culkin. One day, I want to marry him.' My dad, who avoids emotion like it's a skunk's fart, looked almost fatigued by the news, as if it being raised was an utter imposition to his dinner schedule. Ramy started playing on his Game Boy – I would have done the same to be honest – while my mother looked stunned, tears brimming in her eyes, as if this was the most shocking, dangerous thing she had ever heard.

Majid looked to his son (let's call him Hassan), who had clearly been briefed on this Iraqi episode of *Jeremy Kyle*. 'Listen dude,' Hassan chimed in, 'just 'coz you think a guy is cool and you want to hang out with him, doesn't mean you're in love with him. Dudes can't be in love with other dudes, it's *haram*.'

'Exactly,' said Majid, with a self-satisfied grimace that even today makes me want to go back in time and whack his face with a slab of raw tuna. 'You just want Macaulay Culkin to be your best friend. You didn't know what you were saying – you were being stupid.'

With Lily's eyes now fused to the ground, my dad sinking into the sofa as if it were quicksand, and my mother wearing the expression of a traumatised soldier just returned from war, I decided just to say this: 'Yes. I was being stupid. I didn't know what I was saying.'

I said I wasn't hungry, and retreated to my room upstairs. My mother swiftly followed, barged in, and with more terror than rage in her demeanour, held my face in her hands and said this: 'Never say anything to anyone about being in love with a man ever again – have you no shame? Look how you've embarrassed me. *Haram* on you, Amrou!" Her fake nails indented my arm's soft flesh, and I burst out crying and released myself from her grip.

This was the first time in my life that I had ever willingly renounced her embrace.

I locked myself in the nearest bathroom and stayed in there for what must have been at least two hours. But in those two hours, the entire wiring of my brain changed, as if the experience had torn down the remaining neurological systems built on trust and hope. The final childhood bridges were being burnt, with new, coarser and more corrosive patterns of thinking emerging from the rubble. It was the first significant realisation I had that my life was going to be difficult. Islamic attitudes towards homosexuality had already made me feel full of fear and shame on the inside, but this was the first moment that these fears played out in the external world I inhabited. I had developed a mechanism for coping with my anxieties in private, but as I cried in the bathroom, the looming journey into adulthood seemed unimaginably treacherous. And treacherous because of the desires and feelings that lived inside of *me* – as if my natural urges were building the hurdles that were going to trip me up. The enormity of it all fatigued me, and so I lay my head on the cold marble tiles of the bathroom. I closed my eyes and willed Robin Hood – fox, man, whoever was available – to come lie next to me. Only this time he appeared like a thin apparition, barely present, and unlike on our first encounter, the marble stayed freezing, and the world was cold and lonely.

After the Macaulay incident, the colours of my world changed – spell-binding hues of emerald, sapphire and ruby dulled into a formless mud. What was more, I soon realised this mud was a minefield. One incident was particularly unsettling.

During our London trip, I was of course desperate to go to the West End. More specifically, I wanted to see what I believed was the most profound work known to human-kind – *CATS*. Finally, the opportunity arose. It was decided that Ramy, my mother and I would go with another Middle-Eastern family who were also having a summer in London. The two boys were friends of mine and Ramy's from Dubai, and their mother was one of the wealthiest people I've ever encountered. She turned up in chinchilla – even though it was summer – and strangled by a diamond choker that looked more like a neck brace. It was fun to watch her and my mother gossip. Imagine *All About Eve*, but cast entirely by the Arab elite who eat macaroons at Harrods, and you might get a sense of their dynamic.

On the way to the show, we had to walk through Soho. This was before gentrification, and on a Friday night it was gay and raucous and colourful as fuck. I was overwhelmed by the number of outwardly gay bodies, my field of vision a collage of men kissing men, and women kissing women, a street boasting a whole spectrum of genders. I tried, as much as possible, to keep my head down to avoid my mother catching me looking – *maybe if I just stop looking for ever, I'll eventually be straight?* With my eyes glued to my shoes, taking one step after the other as we slalomed through the queer scrum, one of the young boys from the other family shouted, 'Look Mama! There are two men kissing!' *Yes, thank you mate, I was trying to ignore it.* His mother, whose heels were quivering on the Soho cobbles, responded with: 'It's disgusting, isn't it? Don't you think it's disgusting? Every single one of them should be shot.'

Hearing that, I felt as though I was taking a bullet myself. When I looked up to see Mama's response, she was smiling, walking along with her girlfriend as if they were having an everyday, pleasant conversation. *If I turn out gay, Mama would rather I was shot dead.* It seemed that everything developing inside me was bringing with it diabolical consequences. My simple desire to kiss a boy from a movie could result in me being gunned down, and then having to nurse the gunshot wound with boiling water in the afterlife. It felt a bit like having an autoimmune disease, as though my own body and mind were attacking themselves, as if the world I inhabited was trying to kill me for existing within it. My brain was being programmed to fight its own natural curiosities, and it was turning my head into a war zone.

I spent the entire production of *CATS*, my long-awaited beacon of hope, trying to avert my gaze from the spandex of the male cats. Rather than relishing the details of a show that I knew and loved so intimately, I sat there miserably, seeing only damning temptations. I remember very little about the actual production. The only clear memory I have is of looking at my mother during it and speculating: *If she had a gun and found out I was gay – would she shoot me?* For a very long time, a little part of me always believed that she would.

Another thing that made this all even more horrific was that in Islam class, we had also been taught that if we had more sins on our left shoulder than good deeds on our right by the time we died, not only would we be sentenced to eternal torture, but so would our mothers for failing us. *No pressure.* By the age of eleven, I knew hell was a certainty, and to calm the guilt of bringing my mother down with me, it helped to see her as someone who deserved to go to hell. It was a lose–lose situation, granted, but I needed a narrative that would stop me feeling like the root of all evil. As a survival tactic, I began to mythologise my parents as dragons that I needed to slay so I could live freely as an adult – I was definitely going to burn in the afterlife, but at least I could be some sort of hero here on earth. *Picture them as villains, and you'll no longer be the kid in the wrong.* That was my only coping mechanism. And then I found something that convinced me that Mama was indeed planning to shoot me down.

My mother, as she rushed out of the house one day, left a copy of the book she was reading on the living-room table: *A Child Called It.* The book, in case you've not heard of it, is an autobiographical account by Dave Pelzer of his mother's brutal and nightmarish abuse of him as a young child (when he was, somewhat eerily, a similar age to me when I found it). I read it from cover to cover in one gut-stirring sitting, feasting on the tales of a mother stabbing her son, forcing bleach down his throat, and gassing him with Clorox in a bathroom. *Maybe Mama's planning on doing the same to me to get the gay out? Am I her child called It?* As I read it, I visualised all the torturous assaults taking place in our house, and pretty swiftly every room was a psychological site of Mama's potential abuse. This might sound odd, but the book was a comfort for me; it confirmed that my mother could be a woman plotting my murder. The book was like a ghost coming to tell me that it wasn't all my fault, that it was others who were causing my pain. The child is a total survivor, and he ultimately triumphs in a world violently against him. Perhaps I projected myself onto his narrative, telling myself I would eventually get out of a household that might have me shot for my sexuality. Or maybe I felt deep down that I deserved this kind of abuse from my mother, and wanted to believe that she really did see me as A Child Called It; painful as the thought was, at least it was simpler than questioning how Mama could love me even if the deepest part of me was something she hated. Either way, when I put down the book and returned it to the place my mother had left it, I went to the bathroom, locked the door, and lay on the cold marble floor again, imagining Mama through the door trying to gas me with Clorox fumes. After I got up, I washed my face in hot water, like a soldier readying myself for combat. I was going to get out of this a survivor.

What I didn't realise then was how much my life was about to change. Later that year my father was offered a new job with Majid, and our family moved from Bahrain to London. It was time to find some armour; for I was about to enter a whole new battlefield.

THE IRAQI COMES TO LONDON: A STRANGE CASE OF JEKYLL AND HYDE

When I was thirteen, I made one of the most important decisions of my life. The memory of making it
is so vivid that every detail of the room I was in and what
I was feeling when I made it remains clear.

It was 8 p.m., and I was sitting on the floor of our living
room in Chiswick. Since coming to London, I had felt a
heaviness and general malaise, and I had fallen behind with
my homework that term. I needed to hand in a backlog of
three English assignments for the next morning. I retrieved
the brand-new exercise book from my backpack – the front
cover was mauve, of a tone not that dissimilar to my mother's old work pencil-skirt – and I stared at the blank pages,
daunted and unwilling. My mother was on the couch
furthest away from me, glued to yet another Egyptian TV
show (you can take the girl out of the Middle East …). My
eyes moved between her, the TV, and my blank page, each

one a hostile prospect. My mother now comfortably assumed the role of villain in my head (I was her Child Called It); Arab TV brought with it the soundscape from the warnings of hell in Islam class; and the blank pages in front of me were a further indication of my failings. But as I looked at the open exercise book, I had a realisation: these blank pages were also an opportunity to rewrite my narrative, to start completely afresh, on my own terms, with a total, uninhibited agency. I had no control over my burgeoning queer desires, nor my family's attempts to police them. But with this homework, this mauve exercise book, these blank pages, I could control my fate. With the clarity of perfectly clean glass, I knew what I had to do: *I am going to do amazingly at school.* The decision was made, almost as if I had never believed in anything else. *I can control how hard I work at school. If I get 100 per cent in everything, then maybe I won't feel wrong any more. And even if my family think I'm wrong, I'll have proof that I'm not because I'll get straight As.*

I picked up the exercise book, retreated to my room, and went above and beyond for all three pieces of homework. With the neatest handwriting my black-ink fountain pen could conjure, I completed the three best pieces of work in my school career up till that point: a comprehension exercise on *Treasure Island*, in which I answered every one-mark question with an essay; an actual essay about some poems we had been reading, for which I went beyond the parameters of the question, citing every other poem from the anthology; and an example of a 'formal letter', which was so extraordinarily well presented it looked like a bit of museum calligraphy preserved from the Elizabethan era. I worked throughout the night, and my focus never faltered.

Even though I was tired the next day, I felt a sense of hope as I handed in my opus. At the end of the week, our English teacher (let's call her Ms Clare) – a dainty, sweet-ly-spoken American lady with a perfect, bouncy bob – asked us to come to the front of the class to collect our homework, as was the routine every Friday. On the procession to her desk, I felt as if I was preparing to meet Allah on Judgement Day.

As she handed me my fate, Ms Clare winked at me. *I wonder if Allah winks at people who get into Heaven on Judgement Day?* The wink comforted me only for a moment; my negative thought patterns didn't let me believe it was something good, and I immediately assumed she must have had something in her eye. Well, that was until she said: 'I can tell how hard you worked on this. And it paid off.' The euphoria I felt was extraordinary – a current of joy flowed through the base of my feet, surging up through my thighs, rising into my belly and all the way up to my face. As I skipped back to my desk with a smile so wide it looked as though I was on a dentist's chair, I flicked through my work. Every single red tick offered a validation I hadn't felt since I was five years old and unquestionably my mother's favourite. The next time I would experience such a pure, unadulterated bliss was when performing in drag for the first time some years later at university; but for now this high was something I needed another hit of, and soon. It was abundantly clear: a hundred per cent academic track record would be the antidote to everything negative I believed about myself.

Pretty quickly, however, the chase for a high became an agonising addiction, with each high feeling meagre in comparison to the one before. My chase for the 100 per cent mark made even 99 per cent feel like a catastrophic failure; if I didn't get 100 per cent in every single exam and piece of homework, then I was a worthless queer who deserved to rot in hell and be shot by my mother. These extreme patterns of thinking led to some maddening episodes of OCD, and actions that must have seemed totally fucking crazy to my teachers and my parents. There are too many examples to recount, but a few stand out in my memory.

At thirteen, we were forced to decide which subjects to take for GCSE. Let's just say, I did not approach the task lightly; a bomb defuser deciding which wire to cut in order to save mankind probably approaches their task with less gravity. As well as the standard mixture of Maths, French, English and Sciences, we had to decide which of the humanities we wanted to pursue. The reputability of History and Geography were no-brainers, but what to choose for my third spare slot? Classical Civilisation brought with it the Oxbridge kudos of antiquity, Art was a huge passion of mine, and I believed it would demonstrate my creative side to universities, and Statistics was an additional Maths GCSE that I thought would show people I was an academic BALLER. *This is the hardest decision I have ever had to make.* I scheduled meetings with each of the department heads multiple times, coming to school early to wait outside the staffroom, so they could repeat everything they had all told me several times already. During the weekend, I called pretty much every classmate on our house phone to hear their analysis, and as I was such a nerd, most were willing to take my call as a trade for me doing their homework. Eventually, though, they all tired of me; their parents would pick up and lie that their child was out even though I heard them laughing on the other line.

So I did what in the early millennium felt like uncharted territory: I *Asked Jeeves* (the camper, more budget precursor to Google). Soon I found myself on an online forum for academic students trying to ace their GCSEs and A levels, and I put the question to them. The overwhelming majority responded with: 'Just do what you like; what matters to universities is if you do well in your core subjects.' *PAH! I'm not falling through the admissions cracks on that lazy excuse. Amateurs!* What ensued was a creation of multiple different profiles, each of whom asked the question in slightly different, veiled terms, so I could collate as much information as possible. Safe to say, I was blocked from ever using the forum again. And unable to make this life-altering decision, I convinced the school to let me study all three – Classical Civilisation in the allotted school time, Art after school three times a week, and Statistics at home combined with extra homework. *YOLO.*

Every single piece of school work soon became an odyssey I had to conquer so as not to feel rotten inside. Even a single page of multiple-choice exercises could become an all-night endurance test on which my life depended. Things significantly ramped up a gear when we were given our first piece of coursework that would actually contribute to our GCSE for Maths. In other words – it was a BIG FUCKING DEAL. The task we were given was relatively benign: we had to follow a sequence involving cubes, to see how the number of visible faces would increase the higher the number of cubes. Add another cube, how many more visible faces are added to the sequence? From that, we could deduce a formula that predicted the laws of this pattern, so that if we were to plug in, say, 279 cubes into the formula, we'd accurately be able to predict just how many faces would be visible. To get an A*, the syllabus required that after we completed the set assignment, we should try to invent one additional variable to the existing exercise – perhaps one side of each cube being red – to demonstrate our capacity to apply the rules of the exercise to a slightly different problem. I'll repeat: the syllabus required that we only do this ONCE, and that the workings could be summarised on a SINGLE PAGE. I, wanting to ensure that I did everything in my power to obtain this critical A*, did not just do one additional sequence. Oh no. I did 123 additional variations of the event. For the course of the two weeks, I pulled an all-nighter every single night to be able to meet the expectations of this self-imposed and totally futile task. And on the day we had to hand in the work, as every other member in the class handed in a neatly ordered slim plastic sleeve with their coursework, I arrived with a package of nearly 200 pages. My maths teacher – let's call him Mr Brute (it suits him) – stared down at me as if I were presenting him with leather anal beads instead of coursework, lifted the dense wad of workings from my hands, and shook his head. As I trudged back to my seat, I heard him muttering something I couldn't make out.

But poor Mr Brute hadn't seen the last of me. For the rest of the week, I read through my coursework/PhD on cubes every night at home, becoming incredibly distressed whenever I spotted a spelling or grammar error; and every morning I would arrive early to school so I could badger Mr Brute in the staffroom and swap out the pages containing the offending mistakes with the new ones that I'd printed. By the end of the week, the look in his eyes had gone from terrified to pitying, and eventually to seriously concerned. As I hunched over on the floor by his desk, replacing pages with the quivering fragility of a drug-pumped lab rat, he looked at me and said: 'Jesus, Amrou. You must have worked really hard on that.' *Yes, Mr Brute. You could say that.*

Maths, of course, could easily trigger my obsessive compulsions. But my quest for 100 per cent became far more emotional – even political – when it came to English. For while Maths is a universal subject detached from identity, I was an Arab outsider who was distinctly *not* English. As an immigrant in the UK, you walk around with an inherent sense of displacement. This is especially the case when you're a *recent* immigrant, when every street you walk down feels like a foreign land where you don't have currency. While my brother went to an international school, I was at a popular London day school populated overwhelmingly by white students, who seemed to be equipped with a different set of cultural idioms than I was. For instance, I remember being taken aback on learning that their parents allowed them to travel to school by public transport – this, according to my mother, was 'child abuse'. They also swore, and talked of drinking alcohol, and many people in my year group were dating each other, even recounting sexual experimentations. I never swore because of the sins it would accumulate (I barely heard any grown-up swear in the Middle East); I didn't drink because I was still culturally a Muslim; and sex … well, I'd once fucked a marble floor while imagining it was a male cartoon fox. But actual physical intimacy with another human being – *are you kidding?* My English, compared to everyone else's in my class, was of a far less urban register, even inauthentic. I spoke fluently because the Middle Eastern schools I had attended followed the British curriculum, but my accent was distinctly international, with a soft hint of American, and I sounded like a total imposter whenever I mimicked the other students with any of their phrases: 'safe blad' – the cool boys greeted each other with this; 'pulling' – which meant 'snogging' (which meant kissing); or 'sick', which I believed to be an insult, when in fact it meant something was amazing.

There were some other Arab students at the school – three in my year group – and I tried to befriend them. During Ramadan, we all inevitably hung around together as the white contingent of the school ate in the cafeteria, but I was quickly ostracised by them. The three boys saw themselves as tough sub-cultural gangsters, and my limp wrists immediately excluded me from the poker table. In case you haven't already worked it out, I was a very effeminate boy – even an ant could have told you I was gay – and so I was exiled from this male Muslim cluster for being, to use their vocabulary, a 'faggot'. To be taunted by the only other Arabs in the school took its toll, and so I believed that a mastery of the English language would give me a chance of integrating into the school's mainstream cultural contingent.

This feeling intensified in 2003, when I was thirteen. For 2003 was of course the year that Britain joined forces with America to invade Iraq, the country my family is from. There was little discussion of it among my peers, and in truth, I was also disengaged, even though I could hear the tremor of bombs in the background when I spoke to my grandmother in Baghdad. All I knew was this: Iraq was the baddy, and Britain, which was now my home, was the goody. With an aching desire for a place to belong, and having learnt time and time again that Arabs didn't want me, I believed that an A* in English would effectively qualify as my citizenship test. I spent most weekends reading my way through the British literary canon, from Austen and Brontë to Shakespeare (and yes, a dose of J K Rowling). I ingested the words of the English literary greats – it was like undergoing cultural conversion therapy – so that my right to speak it could not be called into question. Whenever I slipped up, I punished myself harshly.

Again, it was coursework that was to be my undoing. The first assignment was for us to write a short story (mine was about a boy who ran away from his family, only to get lost in the woods and freeze to death – make of that what you will). I had armed myself with a canon of metaphors and similes, and all but slept with the marking criteria to make sure I had this down. We were assessed according to an exam-certified chart, which asked the teacher to score everything from our use of verbs to the complexity of our punctuation choices. (A message to all teachers reading this: if you suspect that your student might have OCD, for the love of Lucifer please do not show them a strict chart of rules to be adhered to. It has the opposite effect of an anti-depressant.) I worked extraordinarily hard on my piece of coursework. I went through thirty-two drafts, to be precise, and made sure I had included everything mentioned on the mark scheme I had studied. I felt a huge sense of relief when I handed it in on the Friday before a week of half-term holiday.

When I got home, the always agitated angel on my left shoulder, who prohibited me ever feeling happy for more than a fleeting moment, impelled me to look at the course-work I had just submitted. I read it through, my finger trembling as it scrolled on the desktop mouse, terrified that a glaring mistake might explode in my face at any second. After a nail-biting twenty minutes, I reached the final para-graph, and was almost out of the woods. When there it was. A disaster worse than I could possibly have imagined: I had forgotten to use a comma in a sentence that needed one.

An iron rod of panic whacked my chest. I felt quite genuinely that life was no longer worth living. My first port of call was to investigate why I had been so careless as to omit a comma; I read each of my thirty-two drafts to track when I had accidentally erased it with a backspace. I then downloaded every single examiner's report about this GCSE unit, to ascertain what this absent comma would cost to my life. I then tried to find Ms Clare's number on every school document that was in the house – no luck. That evening, I refused dinner, and even screamed into my pillow in bed. For the upcoming week's 'holiday', I was so fatigued with depression that I spent all of it bed-bound, barely able to eat, let alone talk. I limped through the week with the hope that I might be able to convince Ms Clare – who had said that this date was the absolute deadline –

to allow me to swap in the page with the forlorn little comma.

It felt, and I'm not exaggerating, like a life-or-death situation. Doing perfectly at school was the only tangible thing I had in my control, and without it, my desires and transgressions would take over me like a rabid infection. I was plunged into a low so deep that by the end of the week, I went in the kitchen to look for a knife. I needed to punish myself for this cataclysmic failure. I rummaged around the kitchen drawer, searching for the sharpest knife I could find. My mournful week in bed had completely drained me of life, and I was searching desperately for a way to feel *something*. Of course, the burdened-with-paperwork angel on my left shoulder would not allow comfort or joy to be the solution, so sharp pain and punishment was the most natural thing for my brain to seek out. I picked up the knife, and pressed the flat metal side against my wrist. The cold titillated my veins, which bulged out of my skin, almost asking to be sliced. I turned the knife ninety degrees, so that its blade teased my skin. But my right hand, whose shoulder was home to the angel that recorded good deeds, refused to move. I returned the knife to the drawer, and went back to my bed. Oh, and in case you're dying to know the conclusion of this nail-biting saga, the benevolent Ms Clare of course allowed me to replace the document with the new, correct page.

My decision not to cut is a moment that replays in my head very frequently, and I question what it was inside me that resisted the impulse. Perhaps it's because there's quite a marked distinction between being self-punishing and being self-destructive. Yes, the good angel on my right shoulder was almost vanquished, but some semblance of it was still there. And the angel on my left wasn't a devil, but a good angel that had fallen with sin, causing me to be a deeply guilt-ridden child. It was inherently a good angel. Self-destruction is obliterative and nihilistic – you believe you are worth nothing – while self-punishment is an oddly abusive form of self-improvement. You punish yourself to preserve something deep in your core, which you innately believe might be worth saving, even if it's tarnished, feeble, and almost gone. By the age of fourteen, pretty much every cell of my being was infected with a cancer that told me I was rotten. But there were a few, just a few cells, that were healthy, somewhere. As a way to keep that little cohort of survivors safe, I continued to make academic perfection my mission, and punished myself whenever I fell short, for I had an aching need to show the world this perfect part of me – it was the only thing that contradicted everything else the world was telling me.

This unhealthy drive for perfection is not uncommon among queer people. You see it very visibly among gay men, many of whom are driven by the obsession to obtain the most perfect muscular physique, say. For as a queer person, it is a mathematical certainty that you will be hit with a feeling that you have failed – by your family, your God or your society – and the crack in your being that this causes, however small or big, can bring with it a drive for external markers of success that might somehow repair it. In moments like the comma episode, I felt as though the crack was going to swallow me whole.

At the age of fourteen, I made the decision to stop speaking Arabic. I was never entirely fluent, but I could hold my own in a conversation, understood it near-perfectly, and could read it with relative ease. But my proficiency dwindled the longer I lived in the UK. My mother became terrified that I was abandoning my cultural heritage, so she hired a Muslim Arabic teacher to come to our house once a week. It was around this period that I officially became 'a problem child'.

The Arabic teacher – let's call her Mudaris (this means 'teacher' in Arabic) – was a conservative fifty-year-old woman who saw the Arabic language as sacred, and who didn't hide her disgust at the fact that Ramy and I were Middle Eastern kids with dwindling proficiency in the language. Thinking back to how I treated her, I should probably write an apology note, but at the time she was another symbol of oppression that I had to combat. And I had many tactics up my sleeve.

As well as the time devoted to reading, writing and speaking in Arabic, a segment of our lessons was dedicated to staying familiar with the Quran, and it was here that I really crossed the line. Now, a part of me was still a practising Muslim at this point, but it was fear more than anything else that kept me connected to Allah, and I was questioning many of the rules I was raised to believe. But they were *not* up for discussion in Mudaris's head. I pushed her to breaking point. During one of her lessons, she talked to me about Allah's creation of man. Now, the Quran uses quite a beautiful metaphor, according to which the clay of the very earth we live on was used to mould man and woman, and this isn't technically wrong; every single natural thing on this planet is generated out of something that already existed within it. But I interpreted the text a bit too literally and used this lesson to push at Mudaris's buttons.

'Allah used the earth's clay to create the first people,' Mudaris recounted, a glint of wonder in her eye.

'Hold on pal. Are you seriously telling me that Allah made us out of mud? We're made out of MUD?' I prodded, an arrogant little shit.

'Yes, child. We are created from the earth's mud. Even the soil is Allah.'

'So you're SERIOUSLY telling me that I'm made out of mud?'

'Yes, in a way. And I can prove it you.'

What the hell is she gonna do – pour water on her skin until it dissolves and crumbles? I was, in truth, intrigued at the proof she had up her sleeve.

With the anticipation of someone about to confess a long-suppressed secret, she proceeded. She seemed so sure that I actually believed she might rip off her face to reveal a layer of brown sludge. Instead, she pressed her hands together very tightly and rubbed them, to then present to me the residual debris on her palms that comes when you do this.

'You see, Amrou, that is the mud of the earth,' she said with a look of contentment, as if she'd just solved an age-old mathematical conundrum in front of a room of academics. I stared at her for a moment, utterly bemused, and then went up to my bedroom, only to come back downstairs with a biology textbook. I found the chapter on skin, and began to lecture Mudaris on the cellular structure of the epidermis. As I was doing this, an entitled grimace on my face, her face went red and her eyes the tiniest bit watery. Thinking back to this moment, I'm ashamed at myself for subjecting this kind woman to what can only be described as Islamophobia, and I feel angry at the thought that I used Western science to attack what was a spiritual – and much more meaningful – belief. After this patronising lecture of mine, I decided to embarrass Mudaris even more. I concluded with the line: 'By the way, that stuff on your hands? It's not mud. It's dirt. So you should really take a shower.' Mudaris's face changed from embarrassed to wounded, and then to enraged. She closed up all her textbooks, packed up her bags, and then shouted for my mother. In Arabic, they discussed what a twisted child I was, and I went up to my room.

As I lay on my bed, I was completely unsettled. I felt heinously guilty for what I had just done, but I also felt pleased. The idea that I had upset a sweet old lady brought me close to tears, but by attacking her Islamic principles I was also attacking my own Islamic foundations. Believing these to be in direct conflict with my hidden homosexuality, I thought I had to destroy them. And even though it tore me up inside, I wanted more of this destruction. It felt wrong in my heart, but right in my head.

Pushing Mudaris's buttons like that made Mama very cross with me. 'How could you show an older Muslim woman disrespect like that? Who knows what she's now saying about us to all her other clients – some of them are my friends!' *Aha! So this is about appearances.* 'Everything you do is a reflection of me, Amrou. Do you want people to talk badly of me?' *How have you made this about YOU? I'm different to you.* 'Swear to Allah you'll behave with Mudaris from now.'

'Yeah, whatever. Leave me alone.'

I pushed things that little bit further during my Arabic lesson the following week. Mudaris wanted us to write 'complex' sentences with a list of adjectives we'd been working on. 'My mother's dress is very beautiful, 'The people at school are very cool', that kind of thing. I tried to find adjectives I would most successfully be able to transgress with; as I looked down the list, there were two that offered me the perfect opportunity: 'big' and 'small'. I licked my lips with a dastardly expression and asked if I could read my efforts out loud – Mudaris was clearly surprised that I'd taken any sort of pride in my Arabic writing. I coughed, ever so slightly, and looked at her with an extremely confident gaze, as if I too had cracked an insolvable proof.

'Big. Amrou has a big penis.

'Small. Ramy has a small penis.'

Mudaris's eyes scoured me, and she visibly clenched her teeth, unable to believe that a young Muslim boy would dare discuss their genitals in front of an older Muslim lady in this way. Unlike 'condom-gate' back in Dubai, this time I had *knowingly* transgressed a boundary, and I felt comforted that I at least had control over this transgression. It was on my terms. Once again, my mother was called downstairs, while I went up to the living room to watch *Lizzie McGuire* on the Disney Channel (yes, Hilary Duff's PG days). A muddy ramble of Arabic ensued downstairs, until the door firmly slammed. As Mama walked up the stairs, I geared myself up for the inevitable scolding – but Mama walked past the living room with the slightest trace of a smile on her face, as if she'd just been laughing. *Yes, Mama – I thought it was funny too.*

My mother couldn't keep a straight face when we spoke about my latest misdemeanour, but she implored me – with less rage than desperation – to be on my best behaviour for the upcoming lessons, lest the community should get wind of her filthy little son.

*

During the next lesson with Mudaris, I decided to make her quit. GCSE lessons were firmly underway, and I didn't have time to mess around with Arabic. Especially as I was trying to get an A* in French.

When I'd joined my new school at the age of twelve, my French was very rudimentary. We had barely touched the language in the Middle East, and I was in the bottom set for the class. This, of course, had been a major blow to my self-worth, which rested entirely on a perfect academic record. So for the course of that school year, I had made it my mission to worm myself into the top set of the class where all the French–English bilinguals learnt. I had done absolutely everything in my power to succeed; during the Easter holidays, I had reversed my sleep pattern so that I got up at 6 p.m. and went to bed at 8 a.m., just so I could spend hours learning the French dictionary, uninterrupted by anybody. Every night. For a month. And whenever my parents spoke to me in Arabic, I had responded in French.

This was the final straw for Mudaris: after I spent an entire lesson responding to her Arabic with French, she simply refused to teach me any more.

I worked so feverishly that not only did I make it into the top set, but I won the school award for Best Student at French two years in a row. The victory felt far more than academic. The slow divorce from my heritage was now in full swing; as part of the internal negotiations, I was happy to relinquish the Arabic language – in return I got proficiency in another European language. I was well on my way to becoming a *real* Westerner.

The war with my cultural heritage intensified when I landed an acting role in Steven Spielberg's *Munich* at the age of fourteen. The logical next step after a gecko was, of course, the son of a terrorist. Allow me to give you the context that led up to this point.

Performing had long been a way for me to escape the structures in which I felt entrenched. Academic work provided a quantitative validation that I wasn't worthless; drama was an anaesthetic against feelings of worthlessness. To this day, there is nothing that makes me feel as present in a situation as performing can. When you're onstage, inhabiting a whole new context, you cannot be anything but a hundred per cent committed to the action that is happening right there and then. It's why I fell in love with drama lessons; all fears about going home momentarily subsided, disappointment in myself because I lost a mark in a piece of homework quietened, and instead I could pretend I was somebody else entirely. My drama teacher, let's call her Ms Walker, was a guardian angel to me, and consciously made the drama studio a place where I could inhabit my queer identity. During our daily walks around the field at break time, I spoke to her about my fear of coming out to my parents. As a way to help me, she turned our drama lessons into the campest, most playful space you could imagine.

Improvisation was always one of my favourite times of the week. I didn't enjoy scripted work as much, because the rigorous structure of a text triggered my OCD, but improv forces the performer to be entirely present within their situation and shuts everything else out. 'To start off today's class, I'm going to shout out two words, and then two of you jump in, and do an improv around the words until I stop you,' Ms Walker instructed, winking at me to let me know the room was a safe space for self-expression. 'Today's first two words *are*: hairdresser and camp.' I leapt up, dragging my best friend at school – let's call him Oliver – with me. What ensued was one of the most uproarious times I had had in my life up till that point, as I acted out the role of a gay hairdresser who ran a dictatorial boot camp for failing hairdressers. What started as camp turned into *Ab Fab* on steroids, as if a frozen butterfly inside me had thawed, fluttering its colourful wings all over the room. And the best bit? The entire class was cheering me on. While at home I had to eradicate all traces of my effeminate side, in drama I got to revel in it. As with the dames who captivated me in the British Council panto, again I saw that being camp could be powerful. At the end of the lesson, Ms Walker gave me a tender, genuinely loving hug, and, looking me straight in the eye, said: 'Darling, you were *fabulous*.'

I wanted to be fabulous over and over and over again. Improv was like a way to stop real time, and all its associated paranoia – so I enrolled in a Saturday improvisation class at the Sylvia Young Theatre School. It was there that I was spotted by one of the school's talent agents, in an improvisation where I played a teenager coming out to my mother. The girl I was acting with – and I'm sorry if you're now reading this – was not a natural. Her go-to response was to storm around the room with arms flailing in the air as she screamed for me to get out of her house because I was 'disgusting'. Ironically, it wasn't a million miles off from how I imagined my mother might react if she truly discovered that I was gay, and so my performance turned out to be quite genuinely emotional. So not only did the class allow me to express something I was terrified of saying out loud at home, it also got me an agent. And what is acting besides a sublimation of childhood trauma in order to get an agent?

When I met with this agent, there was, however, a little problem. I had a slight lisp, and my accent was too 'international'. The condition they gave me on signing was that I see the school's speech therapist, whose task was to eradicate my lisp and force me to adopt a dignified RP accent. She was a strict but warm woman, and she impressed upon me the sheer majesty of a proper British accent, how its wide vowels and refined pronunciation signify its nobility, and every week I strived tirelessly to emulate it. I was determined to emancipate myself from the dialect of my upbringing, and to enter the vocal hemisphere of the British gentry. Whenever I fell short in these lessons – a poorly enunciated consonant, say, or a meek vowel sound – the speech therapist did not mince her words: she once called my existing accent 'hideous'. *Cheers, mate.*

Of course, I believed her. 'My accent is hideous,' I would parrot back to her. Instead of fully internalising that Arab culture found *me* hideous, I wanted to exercise autonomy by damning it as hideous myself. And so, slowly, I changed my voice. The soft Arabian whisper became a large plum, thudding consonants all over the shop.

Once all traces of immigrant were cleansed from my palate – thanks, Sylvia Young – it was time to make me a child superstar. *Maybe I'll be a Disney Kid like Britney! Or the host of a show on Cartoon Network? OH I KNOW, I'll star with Hugh Grant in About a (Brown-)Boy – the sequel!* This holy triptych of entertainment never found its way to me. Instead, every audition I got was a pick between one of the following: *terrorist, terrorist's son, terrorist's relative, terrorist's friend, something to do with terrorism, mute refugee, violent refugee, nondescript refugee, Indian person, Asian person of some kind – once, a CHINESE person – token brown boy to fill a scene, a thug, and even, one time, a cold-blooded wife-rapist.* The more auditions I attended, the more imprisoned I felt by my race and heritage. Rather than direct my rage at the racist institutional framework of the entertainment industry – which is not usually so much on a child's agenda – I yet again became mad at my heritage, for encasing me in models of male behaviour I wanted to escape. I had hoped to recreate the joy of the camp hairdresser improv class on the big screen; instead I was doing mime detonations in casting suites. I wanted to explore untapped facets of my identity through the fantasy of film; instead I learnt that my identity was only fit for narrating stories linked to 9/11.

Now, without wanting to go all Rachel Dolezal, I'll admit that the racial profiling of the casting industry led to me experiencing some 'race dysphoria'. The deification of whiteness everywhere around me – and the opportunities it opened – made me feel even more in conflict with my own heritage. One of the biggest facial traces of my Arab roots is my nose. I now live in a harmonious relationship with my nose; it's part of my personality, prominent and powerful, with a camel's-hump bump that tells you exactly where I come from.

Back then, however, I was less a human being, and more a gigantic nose with little arms and legs dangling off it. Puberty targeted my nose before any of the rest of me – maybe it was avoiding my penis, in fear of the inevitable shit show – and it sprang out of my face like a building does in a 2-D pop-up book, bringing with it a whole load of racial anxiety. My nose was often commented on in castings – 'you have *such* an exotic nose', 'your nose is so … distinct', and in one instance, 'your nose is impressive … have you met the modelling agency *Ugly*?' UGLY. *Awesome*. I became so embarrassed by my nose that I tried to get rid of it. Genuinely. During my two years represented by the Sylvia Young Agency, I would wake up each morning and proceed to bash my nose with a book, or sometimes fist, hoping that if I did this every day, the eventual pressure might cause it to push back in. Needless to say, the Flintstones procedure wasn't successful, but I did sustain some bruising, sinus issues, and a rash.

Performing professionally, which I had hoped would be emancipatory, brought with it even more restrictions to my identity. A particularly painful audition was for an advert for a rogue yoghurt brand, in which I had to play a petri-fied immigrant who was suddenly saved by the product (as if a dessert yoghurt, and not a banging asylum lawyer, would be our redemption). So tired of having my race confined to an offensive and limited set of narratives, I decided to conjure a bit of dame pantomime in the casting room, making my discovery of the yoghurt moment more melodramatic than was in the script. 'Ahmed,' the casting director sighed (I once got 'Abu'), 'can we try that again – but a bit less camp?'

'Of course. Sorry.' If my queer identity and my race were two separate magnets, then this was yet another moment where they repelled each other.

Oh, and working with Spielberg … I mean, it was obvi-ously pretty exciting to be on such a massive set in a scene with Eric Bana. But it probably would have been more fun had the scene not involved me walking in on my terrorist father's mutilated body in a room that was on fire. To be honest, I wished it was Ms Walker rather than Mr Spielberg on set that day.

Further shame about my heritage came during my after-school art classes. Oh boy. Let me tell you about *those*. I wasn't exactly a natural at art, but what I lacked in talent I made up for in determination. Art GCSE was an extraordinary amount of work. Each term you were given a sketchbook with an overarching theme – 'the Rainforest', 'African masks', 'Vintage' – and for the course of the term you would conscientiously chart your artistic pursuits around the topic in your sketchbook, with drawings, annotations, and profiles of artists that inspired you. After a term of mining your artistic voice, the project would end with a single art piece that concluded the term's work. For our examined GCSE sketchbook, we were given the topic of 'Autobiography'. Wanting to avoid anything I really felt inside, I decided to do a study of my group of friends at school. We called ourselves 'The Machos'. We were four boys, each of us lanky, gawky geeks. Instead of going on the lash, we studied hard, and had sleepovers where we played Monopoly and once or twice did a Ouija board. The other Machos knew I was gay and were very supportive. (Perhaps even too supportive – for my fifteenth birthday, one of them bought me a very expensive clitoral stimulator in the shape of a massive tongue. There was no way in hell I could take this home with me, which offended him, not least because he'd spent a great deal of pocket money in Ann Summers to purchase it.) We were a motley foursome, complete with a secret handshake and dog-tag necklaces inscribed with the word 'Machos'. We were known around the school for being anything *but* macho.

My art project study of The Machos was gut-churningly twee, and one day our white art teacher – let's call her Ms Paintbrush – mounted the seat next to me in full yogic pose, her African textile kaftan ballooning as she descended. Ms Paintbrush was one of those teachers who was open about smoking weed and talked to students as though we were her drinking buddies, and she tried to talk 'real' with me.

'Amrou, my sweetheart – you know I think you have so much potential ... and this sketchbook, it needs to be really powerful, you know. And currently ... this topic you're doing isn't A or A* material.' *Fuck. If I get a B, it'll be Armageddon.* It was a fight or flight situation, and I was all ears. 'How about you explore *you*, you know?' *Maybe she sees who I am inside.* 'Like go there.' *OK. Gah, fuck yes this sounds exciting. Am I ready? OK, I'll —* 'Think about where you're from!' *Oh wait.* 'What's happening with 9/11, suicide bombing ... turn it into art.'

SUICIDE BOMBING. MY AUTOBIOGRAPHY. SHE WANTED SUICIDE BOMBING TO BECOME MY AUTOBIOGRAPHY. So suicide bombing became my autobiography.

I'm sure Ms Paintbrush was envisioning a poetic exploration of stereotype, racism and identity, but I had a very binary approach to my race by this point. I felt infuriated that even my art had to feel confined by my race. My

'Autobiography-on-suicide-bombing' turned into an aggressive conflation of images from my upbringing and images of terrorism. I photocopied surahs from the Quran and ripped them up, sticking them all onto a page of my sketchbook, then covered my hand in red paint and imprinted it on the ripped Quran collage. And my final piece was an inexplicable horror show, a triptych of portraits of my mother – each portrait becoming bloodier and more decayed – with pictures of the Twin Towers collapsing behind her. Yup. With hindsight, it feels as though the piece was a problematic equation of the dying bond with my mother and my hate towards where I'm from, even though there were Western structures in place that were causing me to feel this way. Handing in the canvas of my mother disintegrating into the ashes of 9/11 only intensified my feeling that I had nowhere to belong. And the worst part? I only got an A for it.

'I don't understand. Your teachers talk about you like you're an angel. Why do we only get the monster Amrou at home?' We were driving back from parents' evening at school, and my mother was baffled.

I remember the surprised look in her eyes as every single teacher we sat in front of gave glowing accounts of my work ethic, my courteous manners, my generosity of spirit, and academic merit. At home, however, I felt a rage I couldn't control, and any conversation with my parents ended in them reprimanding me. By the teachers' accounts, I was a cherubic joy, while my mother saw only a tormented child. Her surprise at the disparity was totally justified, for I was living out a Jekyll-and-Hyde duality. Identity, for me, became something that could be fractured into separate fragments; all the decaying aspects of myself – my relationship with my parents, my fear of being disowned for my sexuality, my heritage, the Arabic language, my faith – I stuffed in a closet at home, in a fashion not dissimilar to Dorian Gray's rotting portrait. The qualities that I wanted to be seen, I tried to excavate from my depths, and to project them onto my artificial identity at school.

At home, my homosexuality was a conversational no-man's land. The fact that I might be gay was never discussed, and my parents acted as if it would never surface again. Frequently – and I mean frequently – my parents talked to me about potential girlfriends from school, and would laugh with delight about my hypothetical wife-to-be as if they'd seen into the future and had a jolly with her. And whenever Majid and Lily came over – every so often Lily would bring a gay friend with her – my mother made sure to damn their lifestyle in front of me the second they left. Through coded signifiers, they were erecting invisible ring fences that were designed to stop me pursuing my homosexuality. Any time I did cross the line, I experienced a painful zap.

One of the most alarming instances was when I used my allowance to purchase a pink silk scarf (which I wanted to wear to school as a high-fashion post-modern turban). Because I was banned from purchasing anything ostentatious – this was actually a rule – I had to stuff it in my trousers when I got home, and then quickly under my bed once I safely made it to my room. My mother, sensing something was up, inspected my bedroom when I was taking a shower, and when I emerged, she held up the scarf in one hand, and the phone in the other. My father was waiting to speak to me from all the way in Baghdad. Even though my mother shook her head at me as I went to the phone, I caught her eyeing up the exquisite embroidery of the incriminating garment.

The phone call went something like this. 'Amrou. We told you not to buy stupid shit like this. WHAT THE FUCK ARE YOU PLAYING AT?! I WORK MY FUCKING ASS OFF TO FUCKING PAY FOR YOUR LIFE AND YOU ARE USING YOUR ALLOWANCE TO BUY THESE STUPID FUCKING EXPENSIVE GIRLIE SCARFS! £!&£ !*!£%(!%@!%)%!@)!@!!!!!!*********!!!!!!!!' What had begun as a simmering rage escalated pretty quickly into a steaming hot assault, and his scream reached such an explosive pitch that he accidentally dropped his phone in the fiery flurry of it all. My mother, who now had the scarf around her neck and was catching a glance in the mirror, looked mildly concerned. 'Well?'

'I literally think he died.' A minute later, the phone rang again. I picked up and it was my father. He hadn't died. It felt instead as though he'd had a sudden personality transplant (or a massive dose of relaxants). As was typical of his intense mood swings, he was now all cool, calm and collected, and, with the mellowness of a Reiki therapist, said: 'So, tell me about the scarf you bought.' It was this kind of emotional erraticism that made me feel unsafe, not to mention confused.

One Saturday afternoon, I heard something terrifying. My father was yelling my name – from my bedroom. Where the family computer was stored. Dread gurgled in my belly. 'AMROU. UPSTAIRS. NOW.' I ascended the stairs with all the enthusiasm of a Tudor queen approaching the executioner's block. My disgruntled father was sitting on the desk chair with his left leg splayed on his right leg, taking up a great deal of physical space in that way straight men unconsciously feel entitled to. He told me to close the door and lock it. 'What the hell is this?' He pointed to the computer screen, on which the Google search bar revealed one of my recent internet forrays – *Queer Eye for the Straight Guy*. I'd seen adverts for this programme, but the panopticon gaze of my parents meant I wasn't able to find a safe window to watch it on TV. And so, late into the night, when the whole house was asleep, I googled it, longing to see men who had no shame about saying they were gay. I scrolled for hours to gawp at images of them, and also to find when the show might be repeated during extra-terrestrial TV hours. There were some 2 a.m. viewings I managed to catch with the volume on only one per cent, my face right up to the TV screen so that I could hear it. How I deified fashion expert Carson Kressley, with his invincible feminine spirit, his angelic locks, and his way of casting a spell on the people around him! How I doted on the kind-faced interior designer Thom Filicia, dreaming that one day he would design a castle for both of us to live in! My fascination for the show was only partly sexual – it was the fact that these characters were celebrated by society that gave me hope. I don't think my father knew anything about the show; most probably he interpreted the search as my ambitions to sleep with straight men.

'What the hell is this, Amrou?' he repeated as I stood quivering by the door. The look on his face suggested he didn't want an honest response regarding my sexual identity; his eyes were imploring me to deny the Google search. He didn't want a confession – he wanted to force me into lying, to make me believe that my sexuality was also just a lie. And so, I lied.

'*Oh*, that. Yeah, that was when my classmate Oliver came around – yeah, he was on the computer googling stuff. I didn't realise that was what he searched.' Oliver, by the way, is heterosexual.

My dad, with a forced grin, relaxed further into the chair, expanding into the space around him the way whipped cream inflates when released from a canister. He then segued into small talk about my day at school, before heading out of the room. As one leg strode out of the door, he swivelled around, and concluded the proceedings with this: 'Amrou – be careful of Oliver.' I knew that by 'Oliver' he meant the part of me that needed to stay locked in the closet for ever. After he closed the door, I felt the weight of the room's silence. It became so powerful that it started to crush me with such a suffocating heaviness that I had to take off my clothes to relieve the pressure. The room became terrifyingly narrow, and I felt a sharp axe of pain inside my skull, as if something tiny in there was trying to claw itself out. I had to close my eyes and breathe deeply for the pain to subside. This, I know now, is the agonising pain of silence.

The regulation of my sexuality was continually enacted through these coded silencing methods. When I was fifteen, *Brokeback Mountain* was released in cinemas, and I knew I had to do whatever was necessary to see it. Once the trailer was released, I used every opportunity I had on the Internet to watch it. I gorged myself on it, memorised its every little detail, with one deeply tender moment in the trailer that I would turn to whenever I needed comfort. After four years of separation, the men arrange to meet up, and when they're reunited, they greet each other with a hug so tight it's as though they're fusing into each other. I was desperate to feel an embrace like this, one so driven by love and desire that it would cause me to melt into my partner; I often lay in bed replaying this embrace in my head, imagining that the hug was so tight that it caused both men's skin to peel off, so that they were two fleshy bodies merging into one complete whole, free from gender, race, or identity. To this day, every now and then when I feel particularly connected during sex, I imagine that this faceless merge might ensue. My teenage years were deeply lonely, and this image provided much comfort for me – as if love could diffuse the boundaries between people, so that we were each of us not separated by our own lonely bodies.

I devised a plan to see the film. It went like this: arrange a sleepover at a schoolfriend's house all in the name of homework; beg said friend's parents to drive us to the cinema; convince said friend that I needed to see *Brokeback Mountain* because I'd be broken without it; watch the film without popcorn or a refreshment, so that my eyes never escaped the enveloping embrace of the cinema screen. The film shows that the parameters of love are boundless, and that no true desire can escape us. It's also achingly tragic, for love is also shown to be something that can be inhibited – in the case of *Brokeback Mountain*, by social conservatism in the American mid-west of the 1960s. A particularly harrowing scene shows Jake Gyllenhaal – God, he was great before he decided to play an *Iranian* in *Prince of Persia* – recounting an episode from his childhood when his father showed him the corpse of a gay man who had been killed for his sexuality. The film showed me things I wanted, alongside things I was terrified of, but it was also utterly honest with me, and it let me know that I wasn't the only one suffering. After the film, I made sure the cinema stub was in my pocket, intending to keep it as a private totem for whenever I needed strength.

The next day, my mother picked me up from my friend's house, and we drove back to ours. She quizzed me on the night's proceedings, and I replied with monosyllabic lies. 'Fine.' 'Just worked.' I could tell Mama was frustrated with my cold demeanour, especially as she'd seen me only moments ago bid goodbye to my friend's mother with all the cutesy charm of Little Orphan Annie. As we stopped at a red light, my mother turned to me, intending to ignite a conversation – and then she saw the cinema stub peeping out of my pocket. She picked it up, raised her sunglasses with the precision of a surgeon, and examined it. She contemplated that ticket stub as though it held the news that she had only one month to live. Then she took a deep breath and made a phone call through the car headset.

'What is the *Brokeback Mountain* film? It's the gay one, yes?' The traffic light turned green and the car engine accelerated.

'Amrou went to see the film yesterday. He lied to us so he could see the film.'

She then remained silent. When she hung up, she put her sunglasses back on, and looked straight ahead. The silence strangled me, and after a minute or two, I couldn't help but ask her what was wrong. Her eyes never left the road in front of her. With a cracked voice she said, 'We're just very worried about you, Amrou.'

Back at home, I was allowed to go into my room unaccompanied, where I studied all evening, believing the limbo of anguish in the car to have drawn to a close. And then came the sound I was dreading – the hollow knocks on my bedroom door, which meant that my parents wanted to talk to me. They stood there like a black-and-white mime double act. *I'm being taken to conversion therapy – I know it.*

'Amrou,' my mother began. 'Will you take me to the cinema – maybe to see *Brokeback Mountain*?' *Curveball. Genuinely no clue how to respond to this.*

After a heavily pregnant pause, I went with: 'Erm – why?'

'Why not?' Mama said somewhat threateningly. 'Unless you think it's wrong? Is that why you don't want to take me? Because you know it's wrong?' *Aha. This is what she's doing.* My dad, the silent puppet master, nodded, and with that they left the room. Again, they'd employed their sniper strategy – a quiet bullet to submit me into a silent heterosexuality.

You know that feeling, when you know what a group of people thinks about you, so you don't even bother trying to correct them, and you even live up to their simplistic expectations, just to save the effort of explaining your complex emotions so you can get through the fucking day? That became home. My parents had given me enough indications that the internal truth of who I was would not be tolerated. So I became intolerable. The repercussions of actually telling them about my sexuality were too grave – I was sure I'd be sent away or disowned – so I began performing the role of the tormented child as a way to distract them from it. And as I was trapped in a situation with so little agency, I at least wanted to be demonic on my own terms, not theirs.

Pretty soon after the *Brokeback Mountain* incident, it was my father's birthday lunch – and I made it my mission to ruin it. It was a Sunday afternoon, and the four of us went out to an expensive Knightsbridge restaurant to celebrate my dad's special day. I was extremely reticent about having to go in the first place, because I wanted to stay at home and ensure every piece of homework was without fault. My mother, as she did whenever I left the house, laid out my outfit on the bed. Every now and then she would treat me to something I liked – as long as it wasn't effeminate – but this time I was presented with a heterosexual straitjacket. As I looked over my history notes on Nazi Germany, I spied the soulless black shirt and dull loafers that awaited me. I tried to kick them off the bed, telling my parents that I needed to work. 'My GCSEs are much more important than Dad's birthday.' My father was hovering on the precipice of fury, but as it was his birthday, my mother was the one to scream me into submission. Before I knew it, we were being driven off in my father's new car, which felt more like a hearse.

So there we were, sitting in our finery, playing the perfect family unit to the outside world. I watched my parents trying to impress the waiters, desperately attempting to radiate cohesion and success. My mother kept reminding Ramy and me how grateful we should be to our father for taking us to such an expensive restaurant; as if by default, all I could tell him was how much I despised the afternoon. Everything I ate, I said was repulsive (it was extraordinarily delicious); any time they asked me a question, I asked them to stop talking to me; and when my parents spoke about how my behaviour would not be tolerated in Iraq, I told them that was fine by me. I believe I said, 'I'm not Arab like you. I'm British.' I also asked my mother if she had ever considered plastic surgery on her nose (which I had inherited), because 'it's really very disgusting, Mum.' By the end of the lunch, I was resting my head on the napkin, pretending to be asleep, and as my father paid the bill, I told him it was the worst day of my life. I provoked him more than I ever had before, knowing that his rage would be tempered because we were in a dignified public space. In the end, my father said, 'Once again, Amrou ruins everything.'

'You've become a monster,' said my mother mournfully. *But I know you thought I was one already.*

So, when my teachers talked about me as anything but a monster, my mother truly was confused. While I comfortably assumed the role of tormentor with my parents, I did everything in my power to be the school's golden boy. Each morning, I arrived earlier than I needed to, just so I could bring the class register from the downstairs lobby to my teacher for when they came to do the name check. Before leaving the school each afternoon, I made sure to go around to every teacher I knew to say 'Have a lovely evening.' After a school trip, I would agonise over handwritten thank-you notes to every single teacher who attended. Before the Christmas and Easter holidays, absolutely every teacher and student I knew got a heartfelt card, regardless of my true feelings for them. My teachers would often comment to the rest of the year group about my impeccable manners, and it felt so nourishing to be viewed as someone innately good. The only competition I had in this department was my best friend Oliver; he, too, was a remarkably polite and considerate pupil – but perhaps more authentically so – and the race to Head Boy had us fighting it out in secret.

When Oliver got wind of what I was doing to earn the title of 'register angel', he too came to school earlier. During term, we would do whatever was in our power to get there first and to grab the register; this sometimes saw us sprinting from the school gates all the way to the register table at seven in the morning. When we wrote our extensive thank-you cards to teachers after trips, we'd compete over the length and presentation of our notes. For Oliver, it became a friendly game, but for me, it was a grave matter. I desperately needed my teachers to think of me as a good kid, because it was my only chance at feeling unconditionally loved by elders. If this slipped, all I would be was the tormented little devil screaming at home.

The double act became exhausting. At school I set impossible benchmarks for myself so that I could pretend I wasn't rotten inside; at home I was a decaying mess. At school my sexuality was almost celebrated; at home it brought with it great peril. Like a cell undergoing mitosis, my sense of self was being severed into two opposing spaces, both of which brought with them enormous pressure. The divisions were only multiplying – over the course of my teenage years, my race was severed from my sexuality, my heritage came into conflict with my passions, and any sense of truth about who I was became completely concealed. This was until I discovered the magic of marine biology.

I DON'T WANT TO BE WHERE
THE PEOPLE ARE

When there were no after-school clubs for me to stay behind for, I would tell my parents that there were, so I could wander around Barnes and delay going home. On one such afternoon, when I was thirteen, I stumbled upon a street in Mortlake I'd never ventured down before – and it was here that I encountered the Tropical and Marine shop for the first time.

In the shop window sat an enormous marine fish tank, teeming with colourful coral, free-flowing anemones, gloriously ornamented fish, and constantly undulating starfish. As I gazed at it, I felt something entirely new – a distinct sense of belonging. Have you ever seen or heard something – a film, a painting, something fleeting out of a car window, a song or a sound – and felt a sudden emotional clarity, as if whatever you've just encountered has always been part of you, and in that moment, both parts have finally been reunited? That's what this felt like. I was deeply stirred by the way that the marine creatures moved so freely; how the soft corals and sea invertebrates seemed to exist without physical boundaries, like warrior shape-shifters; the way the fish regally flaunted their colourful costumes. *That's how I feel on the inside. In my soul, I'm that colourful; my sexuality, my gender – it's free-moving, like in the tank. Maybe my soul doesn't have any boundaries?*

I had grown very accustomed to boundaries. I had spliced myself into different sections that existed in segregated spaces. But here was a parallel universe where everything was fluid. I inched closer to the tank and was hypnotised by the way all the creatures interacted with each other. Cleaner shrimp politely mowed the scales of a fish that was half purple, half yellow; the corals, each with their own distinct texture and colour scheme, seemed to flow as one formless mass with the current of the water. They were united by their diversity, not divided, like I had learnt to become. Out from the sand emerged starfish, along with hermit crabs and snails, hoovering the sand-bed like a harmonious social collective. I was dazzled by the so-called sand sifter starfish, and the way its multiple, separate limbs, each with their own sense of character, could come together as one entity; the factions of *my* identity felt like tectonic plates at constant risk of an earthquake. An adorable cylinder-shaped fish emerged from under a rock, its golden sheen with emerald spots iridescent under the tank's UV light, creating an Egyptian-tone shimmer that reminded me of a dress my mother had worn once in Dubai. And then I met a tube-like structure from which emerged a fan of patterned feathers (a 'feather duster'); it was entrancing, infinitely complicated, yet utterly simple, millions and millions of molecules coming together to caress the ocean water calmly, its texture as silky as Mama's hair. I edged as close as I could to see inside the creature, but my sudden movement caused the feather structure to retreat into its tube. I was desperate to dive inside this wormhole with it, for this new world clearly had so much to teach me.

When I got home, my parents remarked that I was unusually calm – in fact, I was in a hypnotic daze. With a wave of possibility rushing inside me, I spent the evening surfing the Internet, wanting to delve deeper into the mysteries of aquatic wonder. I stayed glued to the computer screen, learning of a universe that was untroubled by the strict boundaries that governed human beings on land.

In the marine world, gender fluidity and non-conformism are the status quo. There are sea slugs called nudibranchs that defy sexual categorisation, containing both female and male reproductive organs, giving and receiving in each sexual encounter, with kaleidoscopic patterns to rival those of a resplendent drag queen. Marine snail sea hares are able to change sex at will; cuttlefish can alter the pigments of their exterior with the sartorial flexibility of Alexander McQueen, and can disguise themselves as the opposite gender as a social tool; while a male seahorse is something of an underwater feminist, sharing the labour of pregnancy by carrying and 'birthing' the young. This was where I needed to be. I mean, it just seemed so damn *woke* in the ocean.

It was at this moment that I began to realise I wasn't fully a man. Now that I have the language to express myself, I identify as non-binary. I like to be referred to with them/they pronouns, which helps me to feel that my gender is as fluid as the uninhibited curves of an oceanic nirvana; when people correctly use my preferred pronouns, it relaxes me, as if I'm being soaked in a lavender bath, making me feel seen as a person free from gender binaries. But when I was gazing into the limitless ocean world as a teenager, all I knew was that its boundlessness had an affinity with my gender. I stayed up late that night and thought about my mother, and about how it was her I most closely identified with in the Middle East. I had so few linguistic, emotional or social tools to comprehend my gender dysphoria back then, but as I learnt of these polymorphous beings whose bodies or colours didn't restrict them, I felt an aching sense of connection.

Gender dysphoria is a complicated and often scary experience – it can manifest in frustration and anxiety, as if your own body is at odds with how you perceive your own gender. When I close my eyes, I don't see or feel my internal self as a man, but instead as a gender-fluid being that's always changing, always moving, liberated from the shackles of masculinity. But when I open my eyes and meet the gazes of others, I'm snapped back into the simple gender codes society has so primitively constructed. It wasn't until discovering drag later in my life that I truly had the power to appease my gender dysphoria. And marine biology, of all things, was the unexpected start of this journey.

I went to the shop every single afternoon for the next two weeks, like a pilgrim who'd finally found their church. The space was in fact remarkably spiritual. Dimmed ceiling bulbs and overhead UV lights gave the tanks glowing halos, as if they were prophets harbouring secret truths. The luminescent patterns on the corals and fish felt similar to those of Kitenge fabric, and if you blurred your eyes, it looked like a congregation in a Nigerian church, with the tentacles waving like arms up in praise. The shop was quiet and meditative, for vibrations would upset the fish. Humans were being asked to learn from *them*, and to handle the creatures with complete respect.

The shop was owned by an uncommonly kind Indian couple (let's call them Anita and Ahi), and in the same way that the elderly librarian grows curious about Matilda during her daily visits, so too did Anita and Ahi begin to wonder about me. I didn't have the ability to verbalise just what an intense experience I was having, nor the emotional resources to fully understand them myself. So I told them I wanted a tank, and pretty soon I acquired a very humble tropical-water aquarium. It became my pride and joy.

There are three kinds of tank you can get as an aquarium keeper. The simplest, cold-water tanks, use cold fresh water, and house goldfish and the like; tropical tanks use warm, well filtered fresh water, and can house more exciting creatures, such as Malawi Cichlids and colourful guppies. Marine tanks are a whole different ballgame, not only much pricier, but requiring scientific precision and round-the-clock attention. I got the hang of the tropical game pretty quickly, and soon boasted a fully functioning alternative ecosystem inside my room. Whenever a comment from my parents worried me, whenever a mark escaped me in a piece of homework, whenever DR. ABC came knocking, whenever a pair of upside-down slippers cost me sin points, the tank provided solace, and as with my experience in improv class, I became lost in its continual present, the underwater wonderland my only priority.

Just like my thirst to climb to the top set in French, I was desperate to elevate my aquarium keeping into the big leagues. My first port of call was to become a member of an online aquarium-keeping forum (my profile name was 'New Kid'). At first, the forum was a place for me to ask questions if something was concerning me about my tank. Quite quickly, however, I became the go-to person for all tropical water woes, and the elation this provided was quite something. When someone would post that their fish were swimming weirdly after they washed their entire tank, including the gravel, New Kid would jump to the rescue – 'Hi PuckerFish089 – it is imperative that you never clean out your gravel; at most you should only replace half of the water in your tank, and clean any debris off the gravel by using a siphon. As a tank develops, the gravel becomes a bed of bacteria to help filtrate the poisonous nitrate, and as such your fish are struggling to breathe right now. Here's what I recommend …' I would scour the forum for any tropical-related issues, relishing the buzz of status this brought me each time. To Allah, I was a sinner; to my parents a problem child; to white people, an outsider; to Arabs, an outsider – but on this forum, I was *boss*.

I needed an excuse to get a job at the aquatics store. As if the universe knew I was destined to be among coral, the perfect one presented itself when our year group was encouraged to enrol in the Duke of Edinburgh scheme. We were promised that obtaining the award would improve our chances at university admission, though somehow, I don't think an aptitude for orienteering has any real leverage. The course required us not only to acquire a compass, camping, and cartography skills – unsurprisingly, I never used these skills during my History of Art degree – but also to do some community service, as well as take up a hobby. As I flicked through the long checklist of DofE-approved hobbies, as if rummaging through a vintage bargain bucket of hideous jumpers, there it was, hiding amidst the never-ending list, the very thing I was looking for: AQUARIUM KEEPING.

*

.

Setting up a marine aquarium is a labour-intensive process that's not for the faint-hearted, taking weeks upon weeks before you're allowed to put any fish or coral inside it. After a year of swotting up, and saving up from many Saturdays working at the Mortlake marine stockist, my parents helped me purchase my prized 350-litre tank on eBay, complete with advanced filters, a hanging UV light (which I had to drill into my bedroom ceiling), a bizarre contraption called a protein skimmer to remove wasteful organic compounds, as well as filter pads to remove any phosphate (which is toxic to sea-invertebrates like anemones). After a week of meticulous assembly – I worked alone; no one was allowed near it – it was up and running, glowing in the corner of my bedroom like a jewelled shrine. It was now time to put some salt water inside it. *Watch out, world.* Anita and Ahi gifted me gallons of specially prepared salt water, which was extremely difficult to cultivate at home. The pair had become my surrogate weekend parents. Every Saturday morning, Anita would greet me with a specially prepared cup of tea – her trick was to soak the teabag for much longer than is usually done – and we'd catch up about her week. I was fascinated by how their family functioned outside the shop. 'What are your kids like?' 'Are they happy?' 'What are the rules in your house?' 'Do your kids wear funny clothes?' 'Would you mind if they did?' 'Are you proud of your kids?'

After my morning tea and obtrusive and inappropriate interrogation, Ahi would introduce me to all the new livestock we needed to shift; from bright blue starfish to spiky lionfish, Ahi knew I'd be able to sell the prized goods to customers. I was extremely good at this, often able to convince parents to spend that little extra on hi-tech filters for their fucking lucky kids. And then there were the creatures that were not for sale. I harboured a particular love for a pair of clownfish that lived in a glorious and ethereal red anemone, which had been their home for over five years (longer than I had been in London). From Ahi – who I viewed as something of a wizard – I learnt about the magical biology of clownfish. Clownfish live their early years with no assigned sex, free from gender rules; later in life, they develop matriarchal communities, where the larger female fish chooses a partner out of the male fish who clean their housing anemone (that's right – the queen fish has a hareem of male slaves). The tentacular anemone in this tank – its gooey threads caressing the orange and white striped duo – was their protector, keeping safe their gender-fluidity with its notorious sting. How I longed for my own protective anemone.

My parents never came into the shop. My mother hates all animals – she's 'allergic' – and my father was usually watching, playing, or talking about football. But on the day I got my salt water, my parents were forced to come inside to help me carry the gallons to the car. Mama, who treated every public excursion like the Met Gala, was dressed head to toe in designer leather and Manolo Blahnik heels. She looked around the shop, seeing only filth. So overwhelmed by 'the smell', and in fear for her 'allergies', she went outside and waited, agreeing only to carry the water gallons from the shop exterior to the car. My father stared gormlessly into nothing, wearing an expression of profound boredom on his face that suggested he saw only containers of tomorrow's sushi. How could he not see that he'd just stepped into an alien utopia?

Our house in Chiswick was very narrow, and my bedroom was on the third floor. When we arrived back with the salt water, the whole family worked like a colony of ants to get the containers from the car all the way to the top tier; my brother, my mother, my father and I stationed ourselves in successive positions as we lugged the huge water containers from person to person up the stairs, like the world's most pathetic relay race. It was very moving to see my family work so arduously to satisfy my deepest passion. For thirty minutes, they silently transported salt water up to my room, and it was the safest I'd felt with them in a while. It's funny, isn't it, the way we tell people we love them? My parents trudging salt water up a flight of stairs like obliging labourers was their version of an 'I accept you'. They knew how important this tank was to me.

Once the salt water was in, I spent hours calibrating the water with a complicated weighing utensil so it was at optimum salt pressure (a specific gravity measure of 1.025, since you ask). I was then forced to wait *three whole days* for the tank to settle, before I was allowed to move to the next stage of the emotionally high-octane process. When your tank is operating effectively – with a salt pressure and temperature that are stable and hospitable for marine life – the next task is placing rock and sand from the sea into the tank. 'Rock and sand?' you cry. 'Is that it?!' But *oh boy*, it's more magical a time than I can ever express to you. For the rock and sand is actually living and breathing, concealing surreptitious sea creatures, an underwater pick-and-mix of marine goodies that will only reveal themselves to you when they are ready. Every morning before school, and seconds after I returned home, I'd run to my tank and hunt for indications of life.

For the first couple of weeks, I didn't get much besides the odd snail or hermit crab. My life was in stasis. Nothing else meant anything any more. At school, I was distracted, readying myself for the failure of the aquamarine world I was hoping would fix everything. Then one Thursday night at 2 a.m., after finishing an English essay, I checked the tank with the resignation that nothing would be there. And sitting on the rock closest to me was a small, pink-red gelatinous creature, moulded to a rock, waving its tentacles at me as if to say *hello*.

As the house was asleep, I was free to use the computer to research the origins of this alien being. After hours of scrolling through marine discussion forums, and inspecting Internet encyclopaedias of sea invertebrates, there it was, a picture of my beautiful visitor. What I had inside my tank was a *brooding anemone*. Brooding anemones are a pretty rare occurrence in the badass world of live rock enthusiasts (we're talking finding Mew in a pack of Pokémon cards – yes, it's that serious). For they are a very individual type of anemone; they are hermaphrodites, beginning life as a female and developing testes at a later stage. They are also known to wander the ocean, constantly searching for new rocks until they find one that belongs, though never firmly settling in one place. There inside the tank was a mirror of my soul, winking at me through the glass barrier, as if it had been sent to say: *I know.*

That morning, it was my father's turn to drive me to school. I was exhausted, but jubilant at my stint as a queer Christopher Columbus the night before. My father and I never had much to chat about, so we often just listened to Capital FM radio on these morning drives, leaving the generic pop songs to do all the talking for us. But this time, the radio was off. When I tried to put it on, my father smacked my hand off the dashboard.

'No music Amrou,' he said sternly, his bushy moustache quivering on top of his tense lips. *Shit. What did he find?*

'Why did you tell your friend at school that you are gay? We've read all your texts.' *And here was the end of life as I knew it. Was he going to disown me? Ship me to Iraq? Lock me in a mosque until I emerged an Imam? Was there an eject button I could press to throw me out of the car like James Bond? (I'm sure he'd love it if I was like James Bond.)*

'Amrou, never ever say to anybody that you are gay. Habibi (my darling) – you will never be gay. It's impossible.

Listen to this advice from your father: even if you feel gay, just sleep with girls, and you will no longer be gay. Your life will be full of disease if you are gay, and you will have no family, no love, no life. Is that what you want? Promise me you'll never even think that you are gay ever again. From now on, you are straight. Swear to Allah, and on my and your mother's life.'

We arrived at the school gate, my face flushed, my heart on the floor of the car, my head swirling; up to this point, all attempts to inhibit my sexuality had been coded, and now he was telling me openly that it was in no way an option. I looked at my dad, who seemed in that moment an utter stranger. I remember being confused that he had anything to do with my conception, feeling that his biology couldn't possibly be linked to mine, that there was nothing that tied us together. I was stuck in this limbo, until the beeps of the frustrated cars behind us snapped me out of it.

'I swear to Allah, Baba.'

'Good. Your mother is heartbroken Amrou. Please be a good son to her from now.'

And with that I left the car and ran to the nearest bathroom. I sat in the thin cubicle, my clunky black shoes moored to the pink marble tiles, unable even to cry, but weighed down by my loneliness, feeling like a stray asteroid meandering the open, empty universe. For the rest of the day, the one thought that helped me through was that of my new friend, the brooding anemone, which would be there to comfort me when school finished.

When I got home that evening, I was taken straight to my mother, who lay on the bed like a withering widow, too grief-stricken to hold her head up and even look at her homosexual son. Her face was swollen from crying. At a loss as to what to say, I went with 'I'm sorry.' And you know what? I did, genuinely, feel sorry. Sorry that something inherent about me could cause this level of upset, as if I were a tornado that brought devastation to everything in its path. My father, who had now shut and locked the door, towering above me like a hooded executioner, then told me how my mother had found gay porn on the desktop computer. *The fabulous cherry on top. Wonderful.*

'The things that I have now seen, Amrou. I'll never be the same again.' *I know, right? It* is *pretty good.* 'It is disgusting – how can you watch these horrible things. Haram.' *Disgusting. I am disgusting. Do you really think I'm disgusting, Mama?* She really couldn't look at me, so I'm guessing that she must have done. My father, who looked more like Darth Vader at this point, chimed in with, 'Amrou, we've been watching you.' *Yes, I noticed.* 'We only want to protect you.' *By calling me disgusting?* 'What has twisted your mind? Is it drugs? Drinking? Are you associated with any Satanic cults?' *Seriously, how would I even have the time for a Satanic cult with all my GCSE revision?* I of course denied all charges (and I was being completely honest). My mother, who finally surfaced from her flood of tears, tugged at my fragile heartstrings: 'Amrou. You and I used to be best friends. You were my Amoura. My angel. I don't even recognise you any more. You treat me like shit. I feel like you've died.' My mother's Olivier-worthy monologue set me off, and I wept on the bed. I wept so hard that I sobbed into my mother's arms, and then my father's, who cradled us from behind. My crying certainly wasn't intended to be an apology for my queer identity, which is how I think my parents were interpreting it – I was quite simply heartbroken. I was lying on the deathbed of the young Amrou, crying the entirety of my childhood out of my system. Once the collective weeping subsided, my father, for good measure, made me promise to them both that I would no longer be gay, and that I would do whatever was in my power to become a heterosexual.

'Of course,' I said, completely calmly, 'I will.' It was as though this episode drained all the anguish out of me. The fear I had of my parents discovering I was gay evaporated; around them, I was now the living dead. My mother said as much – the old Amrou was a goner. I didn't belong in this family any more. They, too, had died in my head.

When I was back in my room, I went to find solace in the only thing in that house that understood me – my beautiful, brooding anemone. But when I turned on the aquarium's UV light, I couldn't find it. It had found somewhere else in the tank to dock. And after hours and hours of scouring the rock, it was nowhere to be seen. Like me, the queer little creature was lost, and had gone in search of somewhere it could belong.

*

With the disappearance of the brooding anemone came the painful realisation that the tank would not be there for me when I needed it most. And the more extreme the policing of my sexuality became, the further the underwater utopia seemed from me. The aquarium was a parallel universe I could see, look after, even control – but for all its boundless glory, I could never actually get inside it. Even as I gazed, the tank reminded me that I was a mere outsider, the traces of my reflection on the glass obstructing a genuine fusion between me and its queer nirvana.

Eventually, I began to resent it. I remember vividly the night that my relationship with the tank markedly shifted for ever, because it was also the day that I committed my first crime.

While I was shopping with my mother in Selfridges – correction: while I was *watching my mother* shop in Selfridges – I told her that I wanted to explore on my own. Once I was firmly out of her sight, I sprinted down Oxford Street to the enormous HMV store, and flurried around looking for the DVD of Russell T Davies' series, *Queer as Folk*, my hands flicking through the collections with the rapidity of a hummingbird's wings. And there it was, the Season One box set, boasting *real*-looking queer men on the front cover, mischievous expressions on all three of their faces. As if my body were acting without consulting my brain, I covertly peeled off the security tag and quickly threw some coins on the floor. Then I hunched down on the ground and picked up the coins, simultaneously stuffing the DVD down my trousers. I walked slowly out of the store, greeting the security guard with an over-zealous 'thank you!' and a wired smile, in that way you do with club bouncers when you've got drugs down your sock and you're trying to seem 'breezy'. Thankfully, I got away with it. Back with my mother, I walked with a forty-five-degree hunch to hide the bulging DVD in my trousers, and pretended to have painful indigestion until she agreed to drive me home. Due to my 'tummy ache', I lay face down on the back seat all the way home.

That night, when the house was once again asleep, I took the DVD down to the living room for my 'watching-queer-content-at-1-per-cent-volume-at-a-1mm-distance-from-the-TV' ritual. The Season One premiere has to be one of the most radical episodes in British television history, featuring a fifteen-year-old character coming on the chest of an older male stranger who was simultaneously on the phone, discovering that he was imminently about to be a father. Yes, it was unapologetically sexual, but unlike anything else I'd watched, it felt utterly true to real life; I got to see queer male characters, walking down British streets, living gay lives, with all the sexual victories and emotional tragedies that come with that. I could feel myself inhabiting the realities of these men, could feel myself being invited to transplant my desires into theirs. While the other queer content I'd seen reflected my hopes, dreams, anxieties and fears, *Queer as Folk* went some way further in reflecting *me*. I went to sleep, the stirring pulse of the show in my veins, and felt my internal desires clawing out of their cage, getting themselves ready for release when it would finally be safe.

After falling asleep, I suffered the most intense night terror of my life until that point, so vivid that it's imprinted on the inside of my eyelids, its fuzzy impressions always on the periphery whenever I close my eyes. The nightmare was set in the deep recesses of a cave that was entirely ablaze; it had flames in the shape of icicles thrusting downwards from the ceiling, stabbing and searing my naked body, which lay shackled to a metal bed that was white hot. Allah hovered above me, a Gandalf-like figure – except much less cute, and much more menacing – and he strangled my testicles with one hand, bearing a scythe with the other. He interrogated me for all my queer aberrations, each of which I tried to deny. He took the *Brokeback Mountain* ticket stubs and transformed them into a rope with which he choked me until I confessed; the *Queer as Folk* DVD box set had been given the weight of a boulder, which was pelted at me and cracked my ribs; and Allah multiplied copies of the Quran that I had defaced with a bum all those years ago, flagellating me with each copy. My parents were also present, and stood with Allah, painfully disappointed in me, and siding with Allah entirely. My mother, shaking her head in disgust, was then called to face Allah's unyielding torment because of how I had turned out.

The heat of the vision felt so real that I woke up sweating as if I'd been in a sauna, and my bed was drenched in not only perspiration, but also my piss. My pillow was on the other side of the room – I had thrown it there during my sleep in self-defence – the bedspread was on the floor, and I had even ripped up my T-shirt during the episode. I trembled for a while, slowly resurfacing into reality. It was 4 a.m. My brother was fast asleep, and the room was pitch black. I needed my aquarium for comfort.

I ran to it and switched on the blue UV night light. The night is a curious time in marine aquatics. It would be easy to imagine it as an arena of underwater terror, but this is not the case; some creatures rest, and others come alive. I had recently purchased a sun coral, a ravishingly bright orange and yellow organism, whose polyps could only emerge in the dark (whoever came up with the name sun coral is clearly very pleased with themselves). But on this night, as I went to hang out with it, I experienced an acute rush of anger that these polyps were being flaunted so beautifully during my night terror – as if the coral were none the wiser, flowing happily without any awareness of who I was or what I was going through. *How dare it?* I scanned the tank and tried to grab the attention of the two clownfish fidgeting in an anemone I had recently found for them – but they were a couple who didn't want to open their relationship, cut off from my pain through the embrace of their purple bodyguard. This was a universe that existed outside any parameters that I could truly access – even though I'd constructed it – and, as I switched off the light, I went back to bed in the knowledge that the oceanic queer universe didn't have a place for me either.

Like an inert husband checking out of a collapsing marriage, I became cold and distant with my tank. There was a drive in me that was looking to escape *to* somewhere, and the aquarium became yet another sign of entrapment. I was a prisoner in solitary confinement, offered access to an oasis only through a peephole.

I developed a physical and psychological aversion to the tank, barely able to look at it without the temptation to smash the glass. I quit my job at the Tropical and Marine shop overnight, and didn't even let Anita and Ahi know, who were worried about me for months. I stopped feeding the fish. I refused to clean the tank. I couldn't even bring myself to turn on its lights, lest I got duped into thinking that the seductive shapes and colours inside had anything to do with me. The undulating curves of the fish and coral no longer seemed free from boundaries; they had become more like serpents trying to lure me into sin. Eventually, even though the 350-l aquarium dominated the corner of my room, my mind ceased to register it. The image of my mother and father as anything parental was quickly vanishing, I was trying to flush out my Islamic heritage, and along with these parts of me went my aquatic Neverland, yet another place I didn't belong.

In the year leading up to my GCSEs, I worked so hard that I barely ever spoke. I got up at 5 a.m. to study, usually went to bed at 1 or 2 a.m., and worked between 7 a.m. to midnight every Saturday and Sunday. On a Friday evening after school, as I was sitting at my desk doing a timed

English essay, I saw that one of my fish – a gaudy yellow pursed-lipped fish called a Yellow Tang – was floating rigid at the surface. I looked at it with the apathetic glaze of a brutal assassin. Within five minutes, my once prized Regal Tang – this is Dory from *Finding Nemo* – had also joined the afterlife. *What's Allah doing to YOU, I wonder?* Then I saw that my soft corals had rotted, their carcasses floating around the tank like the frozen bodies in the aftermath of the sinking of the *Titanic*. Within the space of thirty minutes, absolutely everything in there was dead. I put down my pen, and with the calm of someone who works at a morgue, flushed every fish and coral away, emptied the tank, and put pictures of the tank to sell on eBay. It was the final confirmation I needed – it was time for somewhere new.

A SEAT AT THE WRONG TABLE: MY TWO-YEAR STINT AS A BRITISH ARISTOCRAT

The aquarium had been my promise of salvation – but it had failed me. What was once a comfort, an invitation into a world where I wouldn't be alone, was now yet another reminder that I didn't belong. By the age of fifteen, I felt a bit like an unhinged octopus, a creature missing a unifying brain, a mess of cultures, desires, and separate limbs, all wrestling each other, with no firm sense of place or personality. I was exhausted, and deeply lonely. So I did what any octopus does when it is under threat – I camouflaged. Instead of piecing together the fractures of my contradicting identities, I decided to erase all proof of them. It would be less painful to assimilate, I thought. If my Middle Eastern roots didn't want me, then maybe I needed to find a space that was the complete opposite to my heritage. After my aquarium died, my aspiration to be a fish was replaced with my aspiration to be a Brit. A proper, aristocratic, period-drama-worthy Brit. But how and where could I achieve this dream?

I think each of us has a secret place we go to in our heads when we feel stuck in our lives. It might happen while you're walking down the street with headphones on, the music transforming a banal morning commute into a scene from a Cold War spy movie, or it could be dreams of a life we hold on to as a way to tug us through our days, even if they serve as no more than a mirage. The year I turned fifteen, Eton College became the horizon I chased. As Harry Potter escaped his uncaring foster family into the warm embrace of an archaic wizarding institution, I too yearned for Hogwarts. Eton, I thought, would be my muggle equivalent.

For a while I'd been researching potential boarding schools for my two years of A level studies. It was imperative I moved out of the house, and I developed the urge to implant myself in an archetypally British institution as a way to mark my ultimate severance from Islam. I discovered that Eton opened up their sixth form to a select few candidates, and after a hefty application, I earned myself a place. Once I was admitted, I became obsessed with cultural representations of the school, reading any book or watching any film that offered a window into the aristocratic orphanage that would soon be my home. After studying countless pictures of white boys in glorious tailcoats, walking on the grounds of a historical institution that seemed unquestionably to belong to them, I felt unreservedly that I was about to go where I was always meant to be.

My parents were more at ease with me going than I had anticipated. I put this down to 'immigrant-status-anxiety'. As a person with a migrant identity, you can develop a desire to prove your right to belong in the country you now reside in – it systemically conditions you to do so. Even though the British government mercilessly destroyed Baghdad – home to many of my parents' relatives and friends – markers of 'Western success' still mattered in our community, for they were a way to tell British-by-blood people that we had just as much of a right to be here as they did. As the first Iraqi in our extended community to have gained entry to Eton, there was collective pride over my achievement.

But in my heart, I knew that I was going to make a clean break with Islam. In fact, in the summer before I went, I came out to my parents. No, not as gay. I wasn't out of my mind. I came out as 'English'. Whenever they tried to remind me of 'where I was from' – say I disrespected a cultural tradition, for example by eating pork in front of Muslims – I would remark, with an utterly unblinking expression, 'But I'm not Arab. I'm English.' 'No Amrou, you are Iraqi,' my parents would reason with me, utterly bemused. And with the certainty of someone just saying their name, I would reply, 'No. You're Iraqi. And I'm nothing like you. I'm English.' In truth, there was a part of me that even identified as white, and whenever I had to show my face at an Arab cultural event, I felt a surge of racial hatred towards Arabs in my belly. I couldn't wait to start

studying at Eton – there I could build a new me. No longer
the damaged Muslim disappointing everyone around them.
Oh no. It was time for the new me: Viscount Amrou
Al-Kadhi – the British aristocrat.

On the drive up to Eton for my very first term, I sat in
silence in my mother's car. My feeble knees trembled
against the dashboard, jittery with excitement and fear.
Deep down, I was mourning the loss of my marine utopia
and the failure of my relationship with my parents. The
journey had a feeling of finality, as though my childhood
was being led towards a lethal injection. I made it my
mission to refrain from all eye contact with my mother on
the journey. I needed to picture her as a stranger, even a
ghost; it would be too knotty and painful to feel anything
loving towards her. I had no room for ambivalence. As we
drove, I had the twisted thought that it would have been
simpler had both my parents died instantly in a plane crash
– it's not that I wanted this to happen, but I craved the
simplicity and finality of the thought. They would be gone,
and there wouldn't be any need to interrogate the complicated feelings I had for them; it would end the previous
chapter of my life. For I really was desperately seeking a
chance to build a new me, and on the two-hour drive to
Windsor, I plotted my integration into the most British of
institutions. This would be the most convincing undercover
operation known to man.

Once we'd entered the gates, there was still a drive through the grounds to my boarding house. The imposing architecture was formidable, in both enticing and frightening ways. Thousands and thousands of red bricks abounded towering walls and pillars, each crevice of mortar reminding me that this place had existed centuries before my arrival. From now on, it would boast traces of Amrou in its continuing story. When we reached our destination, my quaking feet meeting the historic cobbles as I hopped out of the car, the gravitas of my surroundings flowed through me. I was hit by the weight of tradition and history, and the urge to anchor myself within it intensified. It was one of those moments when you see something new and it ignites a fire in you, and you think, *No matter what anyone says, this is what I want. And I am going to do whatever I need to be a part of this.* I sort of imagine it's what people auditioning for the *X Factor* must feel during the Judges' Houses phase. At sixteen, I wanted not only a place to belong to, but a history; a tried and tested narrative that bore none of the chaos of my own. I would start all over again, shedding all traces of my Islamic heritage, and would return to the closet, suppressing my femininity for an image more befitting an upper-class British lad. Easy, right?

My mother wept as she hugged me goodbye (I was stifling my own tears, but made sure she didn't know I was sad). I think she sensed that I'd never be coming home in a way that she recognised again. Although I didn't know this at the time, this really was my official moving out, since my parents ended up returning to the Middle East when I was eighteen. As she sobbed in my arms, I thought about how tragic it was that we could have gone from me burning my hand to be close to her, to now doing whatever I could to be apart from her. I controlled my breathing so as to resist my tears, and we looked at each other, a canyon of unsaid things between us. 'Goodbye Mama,' I said, my lips now on the verge of an uncontrollable quiver. 'Goodbye, my Amoura.' She turned away from me, all but limping with grief, both of us well aware that the son she once loved was no longer.

Laden with belongings, I entered the house. The grandeur of the façade masked a rather dull interior – in fact, the first space I discovered was a narrow grey-carpeted corridor that looked a bit medical. Where were the moving Hogwarts' staircases? As I stood there taking in my surroundings, a fluster of white faces whirled around me, accompanied by the sounds of British mothers and fathers bidding adieu to their little angels. And then I heard the high-pitched shrill that I'm certain cracked ice as far away as Antarctica: 'Mr Darcy, where are you?!' Coming to greet me from out of the living room came the Dame, the matriarchal queen of the house – responsible for our pastoral well-being. She was followed around by her giant grey poodle, called *Mr Darcy* (*no*, I'm not kidding), both of them coiffed with matching hairdos. *Yay! One minute in, and I'm in an Austen utopia.* Mr Darcy, probably unaccustomed to foreigners, took one look at me and growled.

'You must be Amrou. Let me show you to your room,' the Dame whistled. Racist Mr Darcy snarled.

'Good afternooooooon,' I replied, attempting to do my best Prince William impression but coming across more like Princess Jasmine.

'You can call me ma'am or mam.'

'Mum?' *I'm actually looking for a new one, you know.*

'I beg your pardon?! Never mum. *Ma'am.*' *Fuck. This is going to be harder than I thought.*

When I got to my room, my immediate mission was to ensure its interior design reflected the new persona I was going to be projecting. A girlfriend from my old school had agreed to act as my 'beard', so the bulletin board above my bed became a collage of the two of us doing things that British couples do – ice-skating during the Christmas holidays, dressed up for a relative's wedding together, and of course there were a few of her solo, which was intended to give the illusion that I wanked about banging her. Next, I opened my suitcase to dress the shelves with the DVDs and books I wanted the boys to believe interested me. As I emptied the bag, a miniature green Quran, encased in an ornate silver sleeve, wormed its way out onto the bed. Mama had put this in there. This was something she did when we travelled as kids, so that Allah could ensure our safety. Perhaps the Quran's function was similarly apotropaic this time around, but it felt as though my mother was trying to keep me connected to the institution to which she believed I *truly* belonged.

There it sat, sandwiched by a Brontë book and a cumbersome edition of *King Lear* (as if I ever opened this), already turning my bed into a cultural battlefield. With a sudden jolt, I snatched the tiny Quran and looked for the nearest bin. But, as it rested on my fingers, they started to jitter and, as the gold-leaf shimmer from the little page-edges glared up at me, my left shoulder sparked with pain. A chorus of thudding footsteps and September greetings echoed around the house, and I shoved the tiny book under my mattress. Throughout my whole first year, I never removed it from this location.

My bedroom door flew open – we weren't allowed locks – and in came some boys from my year group. One jumped straight onto the desk chair, whacking his legs onto the desk to let me know that he had more power than I did, while two immediately flicked through my DVD collection. The entitled knob who'd mounted my furniture immediately clocked the photographs of my 'girlfriend'. 'Who's this YAT then?' he coughed out, as if his own privilege was clogged into a lump in his throat ('yat' was a deplorable word used to talk about women.) 'Oh, Jessica?' I responded, caressing the photo as if it were a hamster. 'She's my girlfriend! Isn't she gorge? I mean fit. Yeah man ... she's pretty great, if you know what I mean.' I caught sight of my reflection, and noticed that part of my tie was poking out of my trousers' zipper. Mr 'Your-Room-is-My-Office' – let's call him Maximus – raised his eyebrows and shared a look with the others, rewarding me with a 'Fair play mate.' *Phew. For now, I'm out of the woods.*

The other two boys were of an artier order. The first, Alfred, who I'll discuss in more detail later, had ginger hair and intimidatingly intelligent eyes that felt as though they were always hypnotising you; the second, let's call him Antonio, had the look of an affected intellectual, a long, flowing pashmina, thick black square Woody Allen frames, and holes in his clothes that could have been created deliberately. It wasn't clear. They scanned my books and DVDs, discussing their findings between themselves, even though I was right next to them. Antonio found my copy of *Cinema Paradiso*, an old Italian film that I truly loved. With hindsight I see how saccharine the film really is, but I watched it with my mother when I was a kid, and deeply empathised with the young boy obsessed with cinema, so unable to fight his natural curiosities and his yearning for a new world. I thought Antonio would be impressed with my knowledge of romantic Italian classics, but all he said was something like: 'God, this film is so fucking corny. How can anyone think it's actually any good?' *I thought it was the most profound thing in cultural history after CATS.* 'Yeah, it is corny,' I said, and then I just smiled like someone who was high on marijuana with no recollection of what I'd just said.

Alfred was equally quick to dismiss the collection that I had hoped would earn me the intellectual credibility of Byron. '*A Chorus Line*?' he laughed, in the guise of a rhetorical question that meant to imply I had no taste. Most of the other cinematic triumphs got the same treatment, with my shoo-ins *Titanic* and *Good Will Hunting* garnering me little kudos. And then there was *The Day After Tomorrow*. Now look, I'm not defending the film or its idiotic director (he's the guy who made *Stonewall*, which erased the black trans women integral to the movement to platform some cisgender white guys instead), but I've always had a soft spot for tacky, crap disaster films. Watching one is like being put into a coma; you sit on your chair and enter a vegetative state as the film's nauseating production value does all the work for you. They're like comfort food for the eyes. But when Alfred saw this, he took great pleasure in saying, 'God. How terrible. This is the worst film that's ever been made' – *yes, but let me explain* – 'it's actually offensive to cinema. I can't believe anyone with a brain would actually watch this.' And so I resorted to the spliff-induced-Cheshire-Cat-grin, and soon they left me alone.

Even after that difficult first evening, I was determined, and at first I was enamoured of everything. The hub of Eton College is condensed into a small area of Windsor, which feels like a separate time-continuum from the rest of the world. Schoolboys and teachers – or 'beaks', as we called them for no apparent reason – wander the cobbled streets in long black tailcoats, striped black trousers, waistcoats and bow ties, with the awesome buttresses of the magnificent fifteenth-century chapel casting its shadow over the city centre. I was daunted, but elated. By the age of sixteen, I had lost all faith in a higher power; Allah was a villain to me – I literally pictured him as Saddam Hussein in my mind – and my fish tank an inhospitable mirage, an empty hologram of hope. I was desperately looking for a new system to put my faith in. Here was a tangible parallel universe – *on land* – for me to jump into; a white, aristocratic version of Britain that was drenched in a past that had nothing to do with mine. Whatever it would take to fit in here, I would do. I set about learning the school's ideology, eager to submit myself to its commandments.

The houses at Eton are organised according to a strict hierarchy. There is one that contains the cleverest boys in the school – the only house to have *fourteen* from each year – and they are called the King's Scholars. They live in separate, grander, more historic quarters to the rest of the pupils, who are called Oppidans (the great unwashed by comparison). There are some houses with an exceptional sporting reputation, meaning that many of their top year group are selected to be in *Pop*, an elite group of athletes who are allowed to wear any kind of waistcoat they want (oh how I fantasised about what I'd wear had I been given the chance: while the rugby players went for magenta and mustard chequered designs – *BARF* – I'd have wowed the boys with waistcoats boasting embroidered coral reefs). Pop was basically an abbreviation for popular, and if you weren't the best sportsman, overwhelming likeability among your peers was key. When I couldn't get to sleep at night, I used to imagine myself as the leader of Pop, in a waistcoat so resplendent with detail and colour – think *Glamrou and the Amazing Technicolor Waistcoat* – that all the boys would bow to me as I stomped over the cobbled catwalks.

There was a moment where I flirted with the possibility that I might be liked well enough to earn my spot among the sporty Warhols. If likeability was a key ingredient, then I would exude it in boundless amounts. But without the knowledge of how to get boys like these to like me, my tactic was to act like a saint, and never have a bad word to say about anyone. 'Amrou, who's in your Maths class?' 'I'm with Ned Edison. He's really nice.' Ned Edison had the personality of Argon gas. 'What did you think of that History of Art class, Amrou?' 'I think the beak is really nice. And I like the course. It's a nice course.' I repeated the word nice with the hope that it might get me a halo and grant me access into Pop's heavenly layer. But my obsession with the world's most benign adjective annoyed the boys, and when I once commented that the sandpaper dry chicken we were eating for lunch was 'nice', Alfred shouted, 'Stop fucking saying everything's nice! Grow a fucking opinion.' *As if you'll ever speak to me like that once I'm in POP, biatch.* Sadly, the pipe dream was cut short when a teacher I raised the subject with laughed in my face. 'Pop's not really … for you, Amrou (pronounced Am-e-row).' *What a blow.*

Costume perks were all part of the Eton status game. For example, there was a set of achievements that warranted you a 'stick-up' – meaning that instead of wearing just the empty white collar, that felt more like a noose, you were allowed to bedeck it with a white bow tie. Most of the ways of getting a stick-up were out of my reach as a new student – being the head of a certain club, say, an outstanding sports credential, or being a house captain. But being an unornamented nobody wasn't an option for me. And so I searched the little book of information called *Fixtures*, that we received each term, and read of a position that permitted 'stick-ups' – this position was called The Keeper of Societies. Even today, I have no fucking idea what the hell this position entailed, but I managed to convince the beak in charge to award me the title with a very hefty application letter that stated, 'It has long been my dream to look after societies and to ensure their productivity.' I also claimed to have 'a deep passion for Excel', and promised that 'I would cherish the opportunity to chart the progress of Eton's illustrious societies through this worthy administrative software.' And so I got my stick-up. As was the custom, the news was announced in my house that evening over dinner: 'May we congratulate Mister Amrou Al-Kadhi on his position as Keeper of Societies.' A faint sludge of applause came from the house, most boys bemused that such a role even existed at the school, with my year group openly laughing in my face. And even though I never once 'kept' a single fucking thing about a single society – so much so that the Head Master's Junior summoned me in to discuss why there was no record of any single society in any single school document – I got my white bow tie, and that was what mattered. Like my mum, I knew the importance of sartorial signifiers of success.

Apart from the King's Scholars, every house at Eton slept ten boys from each of the five year groups. There were only nine boys from my year group in the house I was assigned to, following the expulsion (or death) of one the previous year – I was the replacement tenth. The year group of the house I joined was notorious around the school for being troublesome; whenever I told a fellow student which house was mine, their faces would relay a beat of concern for my well-being, their heads tilting ever so slightly in condolence. Pretty quickly, I understood why.

Other houses were known for their dramatic or musical reputation, and the school would flock to their productions whenever they were announced. If only I could have been in one of those houses, finding comfort and validation on the stage, a space where I had been able to express myself more freely at my previous school. The year group in my house were notorious failures – low down the ladder academically, useless at sports, and incapable of organising a watchable production. And so the isolated bunch were left to turn on each other like a William Hogarth rendition of *The Hunger Games*. And I was the fresh carcass, ready to be savaged.

Alfred, who we met a few pages ago, became a cruel bully, enlisting two friends from another house to help him with his torment – let's call them Charles and William.

Alfred had the worst academic marks of the group, but was one of the most quick-witted people I have ever met, showcasing his humour by picking on vulnerable prey. Charles was from a military background, outwardly supported the BNP, and read the *Daily Telegraph* every morning. Charles was very racist. William was a devout Catholic, and an unashamed Islamophobe. He had a menacing laugh that was like a mix between someone choking and someone choking someone else and he *never* blinked – literally, NOT ONCE.

In my third week at Eton, I saw a poster in the house for a production of Oscar Wilde's *Salome* taking place in the school. Over lunch, when William and Charles were visiting, I asked Alfred who Oscar Wilde was.

'Amrou doesn't know who Oscar Wilde is!' Alfred yelped gleefully, like a salivating dog licking its lips.

'They don't know who Oscar Wilde is at the mosque then?' William sneered (without blinking, of course).

'Fucking foreigner,' Charles tutted under his breath, completing the hat-trick of racist lunchtime jibes.

Not knowing who Oscar Wilde was – Gasp! Shock! Horror! Can you in your wildest dreams imagine something so grotesquely blasphemous? Was there no analysis of *The Importance of Being Earnest* in Islam class? The boys looked at me as if I must have been educated in a Jihadi cave or something.

It wasn't long before the holes in my renewed social costume were unmasked, and the boys realised just how insecure I was about my background. But this only made me work harder to disprove them. After my time in speech therapy back in London, I had all but flushed out the international giveaways in my voice. But I wanted to make sure they were entirely expunged, and I all but tried to impersonate Winston Churchill when I got there. Every now and then there were unfortunate slip-ups, such as pronouncing pasta 'pahsta', using the apparently not so common expression 'it's raining cats and dogs', and once greeting another student in class with a 'hey guvna!' Having felt so rejected by the Islamic structures that bred my anxieties, I wanted the boys to sense no trace of my Arab quiddities; I needed to belong there with them.

But my humiliation only got worse. Of course, this being Eton, we were forced to recite Latin grace at the beginning and end of some meals, and my inability to reel off the ancient idiom was further ammunition for the boys. My constant verbal slip-ups during the expected refrains in my first term led to Charles turning to Alfred and whispering, 'Does the Muslim think he's in a bazaar?' The whispered joke quickly turned into a house-wide staple about me being a lost Muslim from a market bazaar who had accidentally wandered into Eton. Each night during my first term, as I descended to the dining room for supper, over and over Alfred would chant, 'There's a muzzie from the bazaar', enlisting the rest of the house as the taunting chorus. I wanted desperately to avoid dinner every night, but this wasn't possible – our attendance was strictly monitored, and I didn't want to arouse the suspicions of my housemaster or the Dame.

I also dreaded taking a shower every morning. The showers were in long rows separated by only a thin plastic curtain, and they had to be shared by the fifty students in the house. I had long hair and a body that was more like an assemblage of thin bones wrapped in brown parcel tape; the white, confidently male bodies all around me were intimidating. Not least because the boys in my year group would remove my towel from the rail as I showered, meaning that I often had to run back to my room naked. With my hair and body wet, I looked not dissimilar to a miniature Rasputin. As I slithered back to my room with my scrawny body and sinewy hair, Alfred spotted me and shouted, so that the whole house could hear: 'There's a drowned rat in the house!' The nickname 'Drowned Rat' stuck with me for my entire two years there.

My housemaster – who had a bottom that was as large as his entire torso and head put together, and a voice so posh he choked on his vowels – sensed my discomfort. So, in a selfless act of kindness, he made the decision to help me. By forcing the boys to stop their racist bullying? Don't be silly – of course not! He helped by trying to make me fluent in British customs, and to seem more quickly like one of them. My housemaster had an obsession with converting me to the Etonian way of life from my first day there – he was also new to the house (his first year as housemaster), and I became his first project. This all came to a head in the horrible tradition of 'Prayers'.

Once a week, at the end of dinner, the house was forced to gather around for Prayers. All the students would sing a Christian hymn or psalm, and then one boy was asked to talk to the house about something they wanted to share. When a boy in the year below sang an original song with his guitar – his eyes closed in adolescent earnestness – the boys in his year group pelted him with tomatoes they'd stolen from the kitchen, causing him to run off and cry. (I often think back to this moment, of the lovely red-headed teenager with the voice of an angel, and I feel mad at myself for not having intervened. What was the residual trauma of this incident? Has he been averse to live singing since then? Could my standing up for him have made a difference later in his life? But I guess hindsight's a bit unforgiving – I mean, I had my own shit to deal with).

Each week we were notified of who would conduct the following week's Prayers (Eton's answer to medieval public pillorying), and my index finger would ache with fear as I ran it down the list on the noticeboard. Sure enough, there I was, selected to speak, only two months in to my being a student there. But, unlike the other boys, who were free to share something about their life – a hobby, a song, an anecdote – I was forced to do whatever the housemaster asked me to. Knowing about my acting career, my housemaster had suggested I apply for a dictation competition. This was as creatively dull as it sounds; we would recite, *NOT* perform, two texts in an attempt to convey their meaning, and would be judged by a visiting expert. We were forced to present a Shakespeare text, and I was given something from *Richard III*, a text of which I had no prior knowledge or emotional connection to. Somehow, I made it to the final round, and it was then that my housemaster told me that I would recite this text to the house as part of my rehearsal. When I found out my fate, I privately strategised how I would get out of it – could I pretend my brother had died without my housemaster or parents discovering the lie? It was imperative I found a way, for reciting the text would highlight the failure of both my masculinity and my Britishness – it would be like a public castration. The day of the performance, I begged my housemaster to let me talk about marine biology, but with a smug superiority he told me I would be doing as I was told. 'It's what's best for you!' he assured me.

On the evening of the event, I was so riddled with fear that I threw up in the basin in my room. When I went to wash the vomit dribbling down my face, I almost burnt myself with boiling water. I then experienced something akin to a panic attack. The tap in question had grown to become a symbol of British austerity for me – the water came out as either boiling hot from one side, or freezing cold from the other (and you thought you had problems?). So confused as to how I was meant to wash my face, and fearful of the dreaded Colosseum that awaited downstairs, I then did what I promised myself I would not do in my first term at Eton. I called Mama. In our limited text exchanges up till this point, I had deceived my parents into thinking I was having the time of my life, desperate for them to believe that I had finally found my people. When we spoke, of course I didn't confess that I missed my mother – that all I really wanted was for her to feed me and stroke my hair – but said I was calling because I'd burnt my face in the sink, and that I was in desperate need of her help. And so, on loudspeaker, with gravity in her voice, she coached me with a *critical life lesson*: put the plug in the sink, mix both the boiling and freezing water together in the basin, and *then* wash your face with the resultant tepid mixture. *Mind blowing. Who knew?* I was reminded of the moment when my mother helped me trudge salt water up to my room; although she had never expressed acceptance of my identity, she was telling me she loved me by teaching me how to wash my face. Similarly, I had been unable to share anything honest with her for some time – but pleading for her instruction in the delicate chemistry of water temperatures was my way of telling her I needed her.

Bolstered by this contact with her, I went downstairs to Prayers. The podium waited in front of me, the sodding monologue resting upon it, the smug fucking cyanide capsule. The expression of the boys during Prayers was either gormless reticence at having been summoned in the first place, or the sharp-clawed glee of a crab, ready to pounce on a confused little mollusc. The sheet of paper quivered in my hands, and so I tried to rest one arm on the podium to balance the jitter. But the podium was a tad too low, and I slipped, throwing the paper down with me. I bent down to pick it up, but kept my face towards the room, in case any fruit was coming to pay me a visit. Before starting the monologue, I opened with, 'So, the thing about Richard 3 ...' – yes, I actually said *three*, not third. There were a few initial snorts of laughter, as if the room were clearing its throat for a collective belly cackle. One boy in my year group, who had started to become something like a friend, stared down at the floor, no doubt knowing that if he looked up he'd cry, laugh, or have to shield me from the javelins that were en route. I decided to pitch the monologue up to the ceiling, and most of the boys laughed openly, any attempts at emulating a powerful male dignitary undermined by my camp gestures and cracking voice. When I trudged upstairs like a droopy, near-dead puppy, sure enough, as had become custom, Alfred chanted the now staple, 'There's a muzzie from the bazaar.'

My housemaster, with a missionary zeal, was also very keen that I embrace the school's Christian tradition (though it was 2007 – the year the iPhone launched – it seemed Victorian colonial conquests were rampant at Eton). The school in fact offered subcultural faith meetings for non-Christians, but he never informed me of this (I mean, he might not have known, or remembered, and I could have asked, but in any case, I didn't know that they were an option until my second year). In truth, I wouldn't have gone, because I was more than willing to take his lead here, and attempt to assimilate fully into British culture by passing as Christian.

The Eton College chapel has featured in just about every British period drama ever made, and walking through its historic grey buttresses each morning made me feel like I'd made it. Over the first month, I quickly picked up the hymns and refrains, and even tried to join the chapel choir. However, I was prone to gaffes. When asked to prepare a Christian hymn for the audition, I chose, with complete seriousness, 'All I Want for Christmas is You'; when asked to do a reading in chapel about the land of *Galilee* in front of 600 boys, I couldn't stop saying Galileo, whose *godless* theory of heliocentrism – to put it in context – postdates the founding of Eton by a 150 years. But I was determined.

When I think back to how anxious I was during this period, a kid with legs like Twiglets, engulfed by the vast vaulted arches of the mighty chapel, I remember how willing I was to subordinate myself to an institutional system. Shedding Islam so decisively had left a void, and Eton's imperial status became a new ideology to fill it. As I sat in chapel every morning, the light beaming through the stained-glass windows cast a colourful oceanic ripple on my face, inviting me once again to invest in the mystical secrets of another world. I harboured deep envy for the boys in the choir, who got to strut through the chapel's aisles in their white and red robes, like film stars walking down the world's quietest red carpet. The vocal ability of the choir was very impressive, and, as I closed my eyes, the soprano harmonies against the rich bass bed made me want to cry. Or at least, made me want to *try* to cry. I was certainly attempting to will a religious epiphany into fruition, even if I wasn't actually having one.

Quite often, there was a chaplain who came to the house – an angelic, blond, and handsome round-faced man, who I seriously wanted to bone – and I would make sure he caught me reading the Bible that had been left in my room for when I first arrived. I accosted him one evening, and told him that I was desperate to convert to Christianity. But rather than celebrate his latest recruit – he'd won over a sodding Muslim, for Christ's sake – he looked at me with suspicion, responding only with an 'Oh, right'. At the time I assumed that he shrugged the idea off because I wasn't worthy of the Christian faith – *maybe it's the whole Muslim thing?* – but I realise now that he could sense I was faking it.

The line between whether I genuinely believed in the Bible or whether I just pretended to is blurred in my mind; it was one of those lies we all convince ourselves to believe as truth, in an attempt to settle any internal confusion. But when I *really* think about it, it's clear I wasn't actually religious – for my piety was only ever performed in public. I remember once trying to pray alone in my room; I was so embarrassed by my amateur performance that I had to stop as soon as I caught my reflection in the mirror. In front of the other boys, however, I would perform the expected rituals that would demonstrate my piety – every lunch I would make the sign of the cross on my chest (often in the wrong order, as my housemaster reminded me).

We were allowed into Windsor after our early school day finished on Saturdays, and for the first two terms, I always walked alone; most boys used fake IDs to blag pints at one of the local pubs, while I usually found a sushi restaurant where I could munch my sorrows away. But even here, alone, I performed the cross over my chest before I ate; not because I wanted to thank God for a flaccid piece of raw salmon, but because it told the room I was part of a tradition that had nothing to do with my own. On one of those solo Saturday lunches, an elderly Brazilian lady witnessed my pre-meal triptych salute, and yelped with delight and hugged me; we didn't speak each other's languages, but I attempted a profound nod as if to say 'Yes, I know'. Little did *she* know that internally, Allah was pinning me to a searing hot slab of metal and ripping off my testicles – but at least, for even just a second, I felt like I belonged somewhere, with someone. My performance of Christianity was strictly demonstrative up to this point, not liturgical, but this didn't dampen my desperation to 'pass'. And then came the long-awaited proof that my strategy was working: my housemaster asked if I wanted to observe Communion along with some boys from other houses. *Result*. At this point, I had no idea what the difference between being Protestant or Catholic was, and I felt I'd been invited because my undercover operation had fooled them all. I sat with eight other boys, who I presumed must be fellow insiders, each having earned their place in this spiritual elite. They were all serious Catholics, and I observed as they took Communion, consuming the host of Christ's body, and drinking the cipher of his blood with quiet gravitas. When the chalice of red wine was eventually in my vicinity, I grabbed it – since the chaplain tried to bypass my participating, I *literally* had to grab it – and, having memorised how each of my peers took Communion, I closed my eyes, and imitated their general expression of intensity, feigning an emotional gulp of wine, before then presenting my tongue for the sacramental bread in an alarmingly sensual manner. By the end of the mass, I'd convinced even myself that I'd experienced something spiritually significant, and looked around me to share the special moment with everyone else, with the expression of a teenager trying to inhale a cigarette that's lit the wrong way round in a room full of smokers. But all of them were staring at me as if I'd just said *bomb* on a plane.

When the chaplain left and we walked back to our houses, the most devout of the boys, William, held me by the arms and screamed 'WHAT THE FUCK WERE YOU THINKING?' The other boys muttered 'fucking prick', 'rude faggot', or 'disgusting muzzie' around me, like orcas encircling a helpless seal stranded on a limp slab of ice. I was baffled – hadn't I just completely bossed it? The ensuing interrogation went a bit like this:

'Why the Fuck did you take Communion?'

'Duh, because I'm Christian.'

'Oh really! Are you a Catholic then?'

'*Erm, YEAH! Obviously.*'

'Liar. When were you baptised then?'

'Like everyone dude.'

'Did you get baptised in the Middle East then, you fucking terrorist?'

'I baptised myself man. Chill.'

'You're such a fucking liar. Who the fuck do you think you are?'

I ACTUALLY HAVE NO IDEA! is what I wanted to scream back. Instead I burst out crying and ran to my room. The news of my religious charades quickly made its way around the house – my attempt at a new identity now completely foiled.

In the second term of my first year, I arrived back with not a single friend to talk to. Home with my parents was emotionally closed and painfully lonely, and Eton was another ghostly non-place, where again I was having to hide parts of myself in order to survive. And so, one night, as the boys in my year were watching a film, I decided to come out to a few of them as gay. Adolescent masculinity tends to prey on boys who are hiding things; my first term at Eton had been so tumultuous because it was clear even to Mr Darcy (the dog) that I was lying about myself. Such glaring pretences make it easier for bullies to locate your insecurities.

When I revealed my ultimate social failing, I earned the respect that comes with honesty, and the boys backed off a little bit. This didn't change my desperation to be seen as one of them, however – as someone really British, who they respected as an equal. And so my coming out led to a deep exaggeration of my experiences with Islam.

Aware that the majority of my bullies were Islamophobic to some degree (even the ones who would have said they weren't kind of were), I thought I could fit in by being equally so. As a way to earn their sympathy, I painted my parents as horrific monsters, telling the boys that I had been beaten, abused, and even forced into conversion therapy for my homosexuality. With the words of *A Child Called It* burnt into my brain, I compelled them all with a thrilling tale of abuse and escape, so that I could be pictured as a hero of sorts. How could they not sympathise? Even Charles, the BNP-enthusiast, placed his arm on my shoulder and said, 'Shit man. That's shit. I'm sorry.' It was the nicest he ever was to me. *Racism does love company hey?* 'Why the fuck did your parents even come to this country anyway?' he then said with utter conviction, to which I replied, 'Muslims are so primitive man.' William grunted a 'Forget them', in agreement as he left the room (as with the Brazilian Catholic, another lie earned me a feeble semblance of belonging). Propagating Islamophobia to make my narrative more plausible was a tactic that actually worked. For the time being, I was off the hook.

If I'm being honest with myself, this is one of the episodes I'm most ashamed of in my life. To make my own life a little easier, I actually encouraged Islamophobia, and till this day I wonder if any of what I said has made life difficult for Muslims elsewhere in the world. Are Charles or William out there somewhere, drafting legislation, steering foreign policy, weighing up a drone strike, or deciding an aid budget? Do they still see us as somehow beneath them? As someone who had been the subject of such racism at the hands of British boys, why was I willingly invoking more of it? Well, all I can say is, imagine if your life was confined to being on aeroplanes, that you were always in transitory space, never able to land anywhere – the sense of isolation, of belonging nowhere, becomes *maddening*, and you'll do anything to land the plane, even in hostile waters, and even if you have to drown other passengers in the process.

By the time I'd arrived at Eton, I was so sick of feeling that I had no clear story, that I belonged nowhere, and so I rehearsed a narrative of my upbringing that rendered me with more definition. It brings to light an important question about whether any story we tell about ourselves can be truthful – because it is *true* that I had been rejected by Islam. I *did* feel severed from my family, and even if they thought it was for my own protection, I *did* feel emotionally abused. So if I had to recite a story – albeit fictitious

– that would narrate these very feelings, wouldn't it in a sense be true? Up till this point in my life, no stable environment had been available to me; so in pitching my heritage as the Voldemort to Eton – the heroic magical castle – I was trying to establish a simple summary of what I felt. Have you ever thought of what your own elevator pitch would be? What would be the most concise way to explain your position in the world? What would be the neatest summation on your Tinder profile? I think we all harbour a desire for a neat narrative that tells other people who we are, and the utter chaos and confusion around my upbringing made my yearning for this much more acute.

The issue in doing this, however, is that it erases the complexity of being a person. It's like trying to understand a film by only watching the trailer. It disregards the fact that we're made out of many different identities. You're essentially throwing important parts of yourself under the bus in order to save the bits you might think are more worthwhile. You see, even as I basically cast my mother as a child abuser to my contemporaries, once a month she drove up to see me, and I hid in her car, and ate the Iraqi food she cooked so beautifully. And even though we ate in silence, it was always the favourite part of my month.

One day, this contradiction threatened to blow up in my face. Each year, the school held a picnic at which parents were invited to feast with the boys on the prestigious Eton lawns. This day should have been called 'Who-can-afford-the-biggest-hamper day?', and you'd be forgiven for assuming that Fortnum & Mason were official sponsors. It was all chronically English. Among the day's activities – which included getting to play with the school's hunting Beagles – we drank Pimm's and generally rejoiced in our privilege.

My father was away with work, and my mother was forced into coming. I was of course nervous that my story wouldn't match up; my peers would be expecting a woman in a niqab with her eyes to the floor, but instead they'd be met with the closest thing to a Victoria's Secret model that any of them would ever see. I explained to the students that my mother was all about appearances – as were most of the women in my upbringing – and thus she'd probably attempt to hide the truths of our abusive relationship. Mama, apparently labouring under the belief that a British picnic took place in a saloon straight out of a Western, came to the event in Gucci cowboy boots and a Missoni straw hat. *Did she get the idea from the poster for Brokeback Mountain?* I had to hold her steady as she wobbled on the cobbles, and as I walked her to the picnic spot, I felt an enormous rush of love for her, and particularly for the way she treated every public appearance like a *Vogue* cover shoot. Compared to all the British mothers in their sensible trousers and maxi-dresses, Mama really was the fairest of them all. Nevertheless, I had to keep the boys separated from her; the Amrou they knew was an openly gay survivor of parental abuse, and could not be allowed to cross paths with Mama.

And so I spent the afternoon with my mother and all the other mothers. They were fascinated by the Arabian queen who had graced their presence, and I watched Mama do the thing she does best – cast a spell of enchantment. The mother of the one friend I had in the house – a British–German psychotherapist – was the only woman Mama hit it off with, and they sat in the corner like two girls at high school forming a pact. The alliance, as it happens, was against a universally disliked mother of one of the other boys – let's call her Mrs Nosy. She was that kind of mother who, uninvited, sent around pictures of her two sons to all the other mothers, and tried to organise parent bonding exercises like fruit picking in remote country villages. In another instance of Mama being an inspirational diva, she ensured all emails from Mrs Nosy were immediately sent to her spam. You see, Mama used the email I set up for her at the age of eleven, the first word of which was 'cool—'. I fully comprehended Mama's disdain for Mrs Nosy when she looked at her and asked, 'Cool – would you like a glass of Pimm's?'

'I brought my own,' my mother said through her Botoxed lips, flicking her hair and ever so slightly rolling her eyes as she turned to look at me. As it happens, my mother actually brought nothing in the hamper she trudged up to Eton – it was an empty offering only for show. As soon as my mother caught sight of the Beagles, she asked me to take her back to the car – due to a childhood incident she refuses to talk about, she's deathly afraid of dogs – and we sat in there as she gloriously bitched about the woman who called her 'Cool'. I had to save face and head back out to the picnic, but really, all I wanted to do was sit in the car with Mama. I missed the smells of her perfumes, the colour of her clothes, her tactility, her warmth, even when she was being cold; it was a world away from the constipated British austerity I had come to experience at Eton. But then, as Mama was about to drive off, she caught a glimpse of my bright pink socks, took a deep breath in, looked away from me and said, 'Those socks are disgusting.' Once I hopped out, I stood stuck to the cobbles, already feeling a gulf between me and Mama, yet unable to decide whether I could face going back to the picnic. Instead, I went into my room and watched *Finding Nemo*.

Once Christianity had collapsed on me, I spent a lot of time at Eton jumping from group to group, activity to activity, hoping that something new would eventually stick. I compulsively attended as many extra-curricular talks for each and every subject. The speech from a guest lecturer who came to talk about early medieval runes? I was there. The Russian Society play where two pupils performed entirely in Russian? Front row, babe. The rare-board-game members club – you betcha! In this latest iteration of my OCD, I pursued each and every school offering as the potential glue to my crumbling identity.

In the summer before my second year, I went to the British Museum for some coursework research, but really

I was going to mine a new identity. That part of London is a notorious spot for collectors, with everything from rare book and coin dealers to vintage-comic stores and stamp archives. My identity was about as robust as a prismic hologram by this point, and it was looking for any kind of shape in which to solidify. As I circled Russell Square, I feigned a passion for all the quirky collector shops. At the comic store I asked for their 'rarest comic', and was presented with a gaudy little thing in a plastic sleeve. *Could this be the new me? Could I be that vintage individual outsider, who collects comic books, who lives in the curious world of superheroes?* Such was the process as I went from shop to shop, sampling the different identities as if they were clothes on a sale rack. I concluded the fickle afternoon by forking out fifty quid for a pseudo-rare coin from the Elizabethan age, which I kept in a beautiful little box, even though it was quite hideous and of no interest to me whatsoever.

I also applied to be a member of Eton's more exclusive societies, the ones that vetted their members. I tried for a foreign exchange programme to an American school that I had absolutely no desire to go on. Next, I decided to try out the school's prestigious wine tasting society – yes, in case you're wondering, I know how this sounds – and I was put on the waiting list. Thankfully, I knew someone on the inside.

One of my History of Art teachers was a delightfully camp man, who could be spotted trotting to the indoor swimming pool every morning with a bright pink towel in his hand. One of my other History of Art teachers, when not at Eton, wore leather chaps and could be spotted topless in Ibiza with his husband, a former pupil. Safe to say, I collected the ones who 'got me'. Mr Pink Towel was my favourite beak at the entire school, and being taught by him was like living in a Carry On film, a camp explosion of British romp that lay dormant in regular British society. Ever the gay godfather, he got me into the wine tasting club. Other than myself, it was attended only by white students, one of whom was linked to the Rothschilds. It was quite a serious space, and we had to be discerning in our assessment of the flavours. While other boys could shrewdly make out 'a trace of lychee', or sagely observe that 'this wine was raised in an oak barrel', I usually came out with 'it's quite intense', 'it's quite spicy', and once, 'yeah, you can definitely taste the grape'! While the other boys sipped at their goblets like lethargic Greek gods, Mr Pink Towel sat with me in the corner. Instead of discerning flavours, we'd compare what we tasted to works of art we liked (again, I know how this sounds). When we were presented with a dessert wine and asked to assess what cheese it might go best with, Mr Pink Towel and I, as if reading each other's queer minds, cried: 'Why, Gustav Klimt!' It was in little moments like these that I felt somewhat at home.

Overall, most of my time at Eton was spent chasing people and things that had nothing to offer me. One prime example of this was when I got into drugs during my penultimate term at Eton. When I turned sixteen, my father had suddenly made a lot of money. The company that he had been so tirelessly building exploded at a rate faster than anyone had anticipated, and he became a millionaire. I knew that everything had changed the day he drove home in an Aston Martin (I would go on to throw up in it one day, but that's another story). The wealth lasted only two years – we lost almost everything in the 2008 recession – but at its peak, my mother came home in white python Burberry coats and Valentino silk dresses that elevated her to the status she had always envisioned for herself. In the emotionally cold way I had come to expect from my father, he began wiring lots of money into my bank account, the surplus of cash perhaps an attempt to silence my urges to tell him I was gay (though of course I was very appreciative of the financial support!). In many Middle Eastern families, money is used as a tool of parental control; your kids are less individual agents, and more economic investments that should guarantee a return. Whenever a fight ensued about whether what I was wearing was too flamboyant, it always came down to money: 'We pay for your clothes, so you'll wear what we say.' The generous allowance hooks you into a lifestyle where you'll continue to depend on it, and thus all of your life decisions feel as if you are directly tied to your parents' investment. It was only in my early twenties, when I refused my parents' money, that I was really able to explore who I was without them; I have relatives in their thirties who still depend entirely on their parental bank accounts, unable to pursue desires that fall outside the economic familial contract.

In that embarrassingly clichéd way in which excess money often seems to lead to drug use, my cash was spent on cocaine, and trying to buy new friends. It all started during my second year at Eton, when I made a friend who introduced me to the world of London nightclubbing. This boy, let's call him Kamal, was of a similar ethnic background to me, and had a mother as domineering and ridiculous as my own. It was on our walks to and from Maths lessons that we shared stories about our upbringings, and we formed a connection that I cherished during my second year there. Kamal's family had always been wealthy, and he was known to harbour a penchant for luxury London nightclubs. The clubs he famously enjoyed going to were ones centred around VIP 'tables' – these tables cost around £2,000 a pop, and with them came absurdly overpriced bottles of vodka and champagne. Sometimes, these tables could cost £20,000, and I once witnessed a genuinely terrifying man spend £50,000 on a very large and rare bottle of champagne that he then sprayed over the floor. It pains me to say that at the time I was impressed by such a grossly capitalist and wasteful act – it offered me yet another thing to aspire to that had nothing to do with my heritage.

In our final year at school, we were allowed to leave Eton almost every weekend, and it was during this period that my habits with Kamal developed. On one such weekend, he invited me onto his nightclub table. I stood sheepishly behind Kamal as we waited in the queue outside the club, terrified that I might be rejected for not having an ID, or for looking like Gollum when everyone around me looked like deities. But no questions were asked, the velvet ropes were lifted, and we were led through the club-proletariat and into a sectioned-off corner reserved for the gods. In this constructed Olympus we sat on velvet couches in front of metallic, LED-infused tables, upon them buckets of expertly chiselled ice cubes. The procession from the outside door to the nightclub's royal quarters offered me a feeling of status and belonging I had long been yearning for. And the only thing required of me was that I helped pay the bill. *I can't believe it's so simple.*

The setting was very dark, the dimness broken only by perfectly coordinated pink laser lights; I felt as if I was floating in space, no longer tied to the structures of the cruel human world that were inhospitable to me. It was a bit like swimming inside my old aquarium, a ceiling of UV lights above the shrine. The deafening music meant I didn't even have a second to think – the only option was to be fully immersed and embodied in the experience all around me. It was like a visual and sonic lobotomy, erasing all my anxieties.

Around the table danced a gorgeous woman who had the physicality of a proud gazelle, and as a thank you for all the drinks I helped provide for her, she took me to a private toilet cubicle where I had my first ever line of cocaine. Of course, I pretended that I was a habitual snorter, a lie instantly ruptured when I tried to snort through one nostril without closing the other, and then when I sneezed with fright the time it did actually enter my nose. But it got there ... and the resultant high ... well, it felt as if my internal organs were being hugged by a benevolent Allah who was full of love for me. Not only did I feel energised, even happy, but I felt confident, able to take up space and talk to people without the voice in my head telling me I didn't belong there.

After this night I was hooked, and I left Eton most Saturday afternoons, partied through the night, and returned late on Sunday before classes on the Monday morning. I seldom stayed with my parents when in London, and instead slept on the couches of the people I went clubbing with. Because I had money, I became popular. People who were never nice to me in the past, such as the Pop-elites at school and London's top-tier socialites, crowded around my tables, knowing that they would be treated to a free night of drinks, drugs and dancing. For the first time in my life, texts flooded my phone asking me what I was up to, velvet ropes were lifted as I approached, and anyone who used my name on club doors was granted immediate access. I had nearly nothing in common with any of the people I was 'friends' with, and spent most of my time high on cocaine having conversations about nightclub politics. And this, I think, is what made me happy. The stampede of self-loathing in my brain was deadened by the constant lines of cocaine and conversations so inane that they were effectively a kind of anaesthesia.

I knew deep down that not a single person there was truly a friend, but at least I had the tool to keep them by my side – money. Once the novelty wore off, however, the prospect of going home alone or back to Eton began to terrify me, and I became known for violent blackouts. Near the end of every party, I would become heinously inebriated, screaming and crying unintelligibly on cab rides home. After I single-handedly funded an entire night for some boys at school, the group had to stop me sprinting onto the road, where I very nearly got run over by a double-decker bus.

The worst episode ensued during a night out with Oliver (one of the so-called 'Machos' from my previous school). I brought him out to meet my new 'friends', and he was alarmed by the way I was behaving. 'Why are you trying to impress these dickheads?' he asked me, mourning the geek he spent his teenager years with. He couldn't fathom why it was so critical for me to be accepted by rugby jocks and cocaine-fuelled trust-fund kids – but this fickle and superficial level of status was one of the only ways I forgot how deeply alone I felt. Him being there made me feel naked, like the emperor with no clothes. My response to this feeling was to down thirteen sambuca shots in about five minutes. Soon enough, I vomited on the floor, and next I was being carried by bouncers up the stairs; I clung onto the bannister, my body horizontal, refusing to be let out into the real world. Oliver, like the beautiful, kind boy he always was, took me home in a cab, where I was delivered with trousers round my ankles into my mother's arms, totally paralytic. When I woke up the next day, my mother checked to see if I was still alive, before then saying, 'What have you become?' as she left the house. Oliver called me soon after and, once he was satisfied that I hadn't died in my sleep, he gently told me that I had punched him several times and he was bruised in the face.

Even writing this now, I feel a pummel of guilt in the gut. *Why Oliver? How could I punch Oliver? The kindest, most lovely Macho, Oliver?* My feeling now is that I was trying to obliterate any manifestation of my old, more genuine identity, of which Oliver was a reminder that night. My past was something I could not afford to go back to – for there was the place where my homosexuality might have me shot; there was the land where boiling water would wreck my insides; there was the place where I was just a vulnerable and weak outsider, with nowhere to belong. But whenever drugs and alcohol took control, the markers of my new identity collapsed like a fickle house of cards, letting loose a rage that not even I had come to reckon with. On the phone, Oliver told me straight. 'All those people, Amrou. They're not your friends. They're going to fuck you over.'

I hung up the phone, refusing to believe him. But as soon as the money ran out – and it swiftly did that very summer – not one of my nightclub gang was by my side. My stint as a nightclub bachelor concluded when I tried to get myself onto a friend's table (one who had leeched off me several times). But without a penny to my name, his friend – an extraordinarily rich and repugnant creature – after complaining that my dancing was 'too fucking gay' (*what's wrong with a bit of belly work!*), told me to 'fuck off'. And not one person on the table sacrificed the honour of a free vodka Red Bull to stand up for me.

Drinking and drugs weren't the only discoveries I made during my time at Eton. It's also the place where I lost my virginity, and I'm now working incredibly hard to unlearn the things I was taught in that department. To tell you about all this, I'm going to have to be vague, lest my story should inadvertently bring a now married man out of the closet. But what I can tell you was that there was a boy with whom I studied Biology, and he turned sex into a war zone for me. Let's call him Mason. Mason was a beautiful, well chiselled, sharp-featured teenager with long bright blond hair and a spellbinding gaze. He was an extraordinarily articulate boy, disarmingly charming, and so astute with his description of things that he'd quite frequently have me crying with laughter. His acerbic tongue gave him a status he didn't get academically or from his extra-curricular CV, and you couldn't help but want to be around him, partly because you knew that if you weren't you might be victim to his verbal bite.

When you were on Mason's good side, you felt like the most special person in the world. He was aware that he had this talent, and he preyed on the most vulnerable – newbies and younger boys were his favourite – though he also bedded masculine sports deities, holding the knowledge of their emasculation if ever they undermined him. Now this isn't just self-deprecation, but I wasn't an attractive teenager. I had the physicality of a broken toothpick, braces, glasses, cystic acne, and long black hair that apparently gave me the unfortunate appearance of a sewer rat whenever I got out of the shower. After the poodle, Mason was my second Mr Darcy at Eton. Mason started courting me because of his academic insecurities; I had clout when it came to my rank in the classroom, while Mason was winning in pretty much all other departments.

Like an expert groomer, Mason's initial tactic was to be uncommonly friendly to me, giving me what so few other people offered me at Eton. On the way to and from lessons, he would dazzle me with his takedowns of the other boys in our class, making me feel that it was the two of us against the world. I was the only person of colour in my Biology class, and my sexuality and new-boy status were leverage for Mason. He would give his time in return for me helping him academically. Mason had been watching me like a hawk and was well versed in all my specific insecurities; for instance, he once gifted me with a list of films that I should watch to get 'cultured'.

By the end of my second term, he was slowly playing footsie with me during Chapel. With such obliterated self-worth, and no idea that I could ever be attractive, it wasn't until we were in my room after an evening chapel service and he said, 'This is the part where we pull,' that we first had sex. It was as if my homosexual desires had been locked up in solitary confinement for all my life and were suddenly out on day release. Our first kiss was less like a kiss and more like me mopping his face with my tongue. Pretty swiftly I was naked and kneeling on the floor, sucking his penis. It struck me that his arse must have been sitting on the little Quran my mother had given me – and before I knew it, come had erupted out of my penis like magma from a pent-up volcano. When Mason saw what had happened, my knees tremoring on the carpet, he looked down at me and said, with the neutrality of a GP asking if you'd passed urine, 'You've come, haven't you? That's a shame.'

It felt as if my body was guided by an external force that was controlling my ejaculation, shouting at my brain to EJECT because what I was doing was so shameful. As I lay in bed that night, the pleasure of the experience wrestled with the shame of it; I had fully yielded to the temptation of the serpent and eaten the forbidden fruit, and my body had prematurely ejaculated as a way to prohibit further transgressions. But, as of that moment, I knew I was doomed. Because what I felt during the brief sexual episode was the most in touch I had been with something that had long been policed inside of me. There was no way I could resist another bite.

Mason seized upon my powerlessness. I wasn't the only boy he was sleeping with. There were many places that we had sex, and one of them was a school society meeting room that had a mattress in it; I would see Mason's boys come and go, and they included the most influential people in Pop, along with many others who had given me hell. The fact that I could be desired by a boy who was already bedding the elite felt like a privilege to me, and Mason reminded me time and time again of this power structure. Like *The Talented Mr Ripley*, he was an expert at manipulation. During a lesson, he had once joined in with the other boys who were teasing me for submitting homework the length of *War and Peace*; but later that evening, when we were hanging out at our secret place, Mason was only a source of comfort, rewarding me with sex. Our sexual transactions were entirely decided by him, of course – often they would entail me rolling over and allowing him to penetrate me. When I was well behaved and on his good side, I might get some kissing, or even a blow job, but those felt like a reward. Mason also enjoyed suddenly punishing me. One night, he was giving me a blow job, and as he rubbed his hands over my skinny frame he suddenly looked up at me, shook his body as if he was trying to shirk the feeling of something 'icky', then got up and left me alone in my room, so I could sit with the shame of my undesirability. As though I was suffering Stockholm

Syndrome, such episodes only intensified my yearning for him.

One of the most hurtful incidents took place during a school play at the start of my second year. The school often brought in girls from neighbouring schools for us to act with in productions. In this production, I was quick to befriend one of them – let's call her Arabella – and we formed what I believed was a true, meaningful connection. Arabella was extraordinarily beautiful and talented, and one couldn't help but want to be in her orbit. Arabella was creative, and she and I had many a conversation about our shared interests. Mason grew jealous. It wasn't in our sexual contract that I could make friends without his permission. And so Mason too became friends with Arabella, and offered her something I never could – a sense of entitlement at Eton. This friend *I* had made was soon enough on the phone to Mason every evening. During rehearsals they began to sit separately from me, effortlessly more attractive and cool than I was. I had told Arabella about my sexual interactions with Mason, because I believed the two of us to be close, and I needed *someone* to talk to about them. But during one rehearsal, when Arabella and Mason didn't realise I was sitting behind them – *or maybe they did?* – Arabella asked, in that way which suggests 'yes' would be an impossible answer, 'You're not *actually* attracted to Amrou, are you?' Mason, who enjoyed being firmly in the same league as Arabella, snorted with laughter. 'Yuck. Of course not. He's disgusting. I do it 'cos

167

I pity him.' The worst thing is that I fully believed him.

Mason's actions went from cruel to dangerous. In my final term, I was cast in the most coveted role of a school production (*bow down, biatches*). Also in the cast was a beautiful and artistic fifteen-year-old boy, with shaggy brown hair and sweetly circular glasses – let's call him Nicholas – who had once been engaged in sexual activity with Mason. Nicholas and I became extremely close friends (though nothing romantic ensued), and I was dazzled by his sensitive understanding of most social situations.

Mason also auditioned and secured a part, albeit a much smaller one. As he got wind of my developing friendship with Nicholas, he asked our director if he could be present at every rehearsal, so enraged that I was becoming close with one of his sexual conquests. It was then that he started photographing the rehearsals 'for fun'. It seemed to me that Mason wanted to observe our every movement, both with his eye and that of his camera's. People often say that the patriarchy exists in the male gaze, and I felt it acutely during this episode; with the scopophilic obsession of the Robin Williams character in *One Hour Photo*, Mason used his eyes to remind me that I was his subject, and that I was powerless to escape the prison of our established hierarchy. Throughout every rehearsal, the quiet ticking of his camera shutter ensured I knew that every interaction with Nicholas was being silently policed; it reminded me of home, and how my parents impressed on me that my every instinctual desire was being closely monitored.

The wrap party for the play was held in Bella Italia – Partaaaay! – and Mason made sure he was sitting opposite me and Nicholas. The two of us designed an escape plan, and agreed to run off from the party the second Mason was in the loo. In no more than a millisecond after Mason had excused himself, we snatched a bottle of wine and ran off, finding refuge in one of Eton's private gardens. We lay entwined in platonic bliss, drank wine, and fantasised about adulthood, and how freeing it would eventually be to have queer lives. With the lawn a carpet for our dreams, we heard Mason in the distance screaming our names, raising the hairs on the back of our necks even though it was a perfect summer evening. As I was making my way back to the house later that night, I walked past the secret location Mason and I used for sex, creeping as quietly as I could. But with the hunting agility of a cheetah, Mason spotted me, grabbed my shoulders, slammed me against the wall, and asked me over and over if Nicholas and I had just had sex. The idea that my friendship with Nicholas was based purely on an emotional, platonic bond seemed utterly impossible to Mason, as if all relationships could only be a constant exchange of power. As Mason's eyes tore into me, I felt profoundly sorry for him, wondering what had reduced him to a person whose body circulated with such venom in place of blood. That was until the next evening, when Nicholas called me, saying it was urgent we spoke. After that morning's session at Chapel, Mason sneaked himself into Nicholas's room and lay on his bed, waiting for his return. 'I ended up giving him a blow job,' Nicholas said, more like a question than a statement. 'Did you want to?' I asked, in a mixture of anger, sadness, and jealousy. Nicholas, now fighting back tears, eventually replied: 'It was horrible.'

You might be questioning why I allowed Mason to treat me this way. I often do myself. But at the age of sixteen, and as someone who had not found true acceptance anywhere I turned, I was willing to accept any crumbs of acceptance that were thrown my way. This, in all honesty, is the condition of being queer in a world that's not designed for you – your self-worth can take such a beating that it's impossible not to interpret any kind of affection, even if it's intermittently violent, as a reward. Even after Mason repeatedly demeaned me, I still felt lucky that any guy FULL STOP was willing to have sex with me. That's how low my self-esteem was. I had come to Eton to build a powerful new me, and while I was there, I constructed a feeble new avatar. So far away from who I was – feeling rotten even in my bones – I allowed myself to be treated in a way I felt I deserved.

Eton, which I'd envisioned as my salvation, the place to elevate me out of my past, was a dizzying whirlwind of torment and confusion. My sexual experiences there have left residual habits that get in the way of my experiencing intimacy even today; my search for a new self revealed that it was even more elusive than I had ever anticipated; and the narration of my parents as Islamist-child-abusers left me feeling at odds with my own reality. By the time I left Eton, I was nothing more than an unarmoured unicorn, with a blunt, weathered horn, wandering alone once again.

ME, MYSELF, AND LIES: THE MANY FACES OF BEING A DRAG QUEEN

During my final year of university, I went to Paris with the queens from my drag troupe, Denim. Denim is a drag night that I started while at Cambridge, and by my final year, there were five queens who regularly performed. We became a very tight friendship group. As its creator, I was the automatic mother of the group, making sure that everything and everyone was organised, and I prided myself for my dependability and for being a pillar of support to my sisters.

As we walked through the Parisian streets on a crisp winter evening, I unexpectedly saw Mason, standing across the road from me, kissing a girl. This was the first time since graduating from Eton that I had seen him (I had actually forced myself never to think about him). My body sprinted towards a cab without consulting my brain, and before I knew it I was pulling the queens into the taxi with me. I was shaking during the journey, shouted quite a few times, burst into an emotional rage over a five-euro hat that I had bought and lost earlier that day, and as soon as I got home, I had to take a nap. Once I had arisen, I went out for margaritas with the queens, calmer and wearing a cosmic-themed cape that one of them had lent me that trip (another item I later lost). When they asked me about what had happened, I made it perfectly clear that I had no intention of ever talking about it. Among the chorus of concerns and questions came, 'I've never seen you like that', 'You never get that upset', 'Glamrou – what was that? What's going on?'

The queens, who had become a true queer family to me, seemed deeply concerned, even surprised, that I had had such a volatile bodily reaction to seeing a person from my past. I'd never once spoken about Mason. In fact, I'd never really gone into detail about my family problems either. With them, I wanted to be a maternal queer protector who was full of only wisdom, light and positivity. But in that instance, it was clear to all of us that my unresolved past sizzled only millimetres under a brightly made-up surface. As a student, I worked tirelessly to ensure that everyone saw only the illusion of the colourful land of Oz I presented to them. The attempts to disguise my struggling behind this curtain are what characterised my four years at Cambridge University.

*

Cambridge was the first place I lived without the policing gaze of my parents or teachers, so I was 'free' for the first time. While Cambridge was an open and liberal place, this was more true academically than in any real way on the ground, and there wasn't a space for queer forms of gender and sexual expression. There were a number of LGBT club-nights and society groups, but the overwhelming number of white male bodies quite frankly intimidated me, and I found myself hiding behind plain T-shirts and jeans to fit in among the normative crowd. It is well known that homophobia exists also in the gay community, and I got wind of this when I joined the gay dating app Grindr as a student. When my profile picture showed me in a more feminine light, I'd receive significantly fewer matches, and common femme-phobic remarks, including 'Are you straight-acting?' and 'No Femmes'. Every now and then I even got 'No Asians'. Even gay male spaces seemed to limit any forms of femininity or non-conformism, and this was an untapped part of myself that was screaming to be let out. So in the second term of my second year, I made the decision to start a drag night.

Besides my efforts as period drama dames in Eton farces, I had no experience of drag, so in a way I'm amazed I had the deluded confidence to do this. But the Cambridge terms were short, and always in the back of my head was the idea that everything was suddenly going to implode on me – it felt like there was little time to waste. If I was going to express myself properly in an authentic, liberated way, then I had to do it *now*. The first port of call was to put out a Facebook post to see if anybody else wanted to try drag with me. I thought I might get the odd like/insult/fatwa, but it soon became abundantly clear that a whole cohort of my peers also felt they needed a space to experiment with gender. By the time the night started, there were about fifteen signed-up drag queens, kings, and gender-aliens in lycra who looked neither male nor female, and even pirates. As there had never been a drag club-night before this, and since it was taking place in a building that seemed designed to induce an asthma attack, I wasn't sure how many people might turn up. But after only a few days on Facebook, the number of people who had clicked attending was close to 400. *Fuck. I don't even know what I'm doing.* To make the night a reality, I had to go to Barclays Bank and drain the remaining pounds from my student loan for that term (which reminds me – I still need to pay this back). I used the government credit to rent out the underground crypt and some microphones, and printed embarrassingly clichéd images of Judy Garland, Liza Minnelli and Lady Gaga to plaster over the damp walls. With the rest of the cash, almost as if on autopilot, I went on eBay and ordered myself a pair of heels and a giant blonde wig (which looked a bit like an electrocuted guinea pig). I hadn't worked out what my drag aesthetic might be at this point in my life, but these objects just spoke to me, like glittery queer horcruxes that would make me indestructible.

In the two weeks leading up to the first Denim, I met up with each of the performers, to talk with them about what they were going to perform and to offer my advice. Odd, this, as I genuinely had no advice to offer them. Absolutely nothing. I was like a character in *Bugsy Malone*, a kid dressed in the adult costume of a gangster, pretending to run shit while secretly peeing nervously down their leg. I was shambolically dismal when it came to make-up; I hopscotched in heels more than I walked in them; I had the sartorial instincts of a confused Amish person in Primark; and I knew nearly nothing about singing live in drag. It felt as if everyone had been fooled into thinking I was some queer missionary – and I was more than happy to go along with the charade. For the first time ever in my life, I had power *because* I was queer.

To cement my position as a drag mother hen, I did what any misguided drag queen does at the start of their career – I sang a song from a famous musical. My chosen number was 'When You're Good to Mama' from *Chicago*. CRINGE. The day itself was utterly chaotic. At one point I had to schlep all the decorations from one side of Cambridge to the other in a wheelie bin. Every single performer was a bundle of nerves, not one of us having ever done this before. But it fell on me to provide the words of comfort – I was mother after all – and while everyone got ready, I watched as each of them had a partner or a friend to help them with their make-up and costume. They all probably thought I didn't need any help, but in truth I needed the most out of all of them. As I retreated to the corner, trying to figure out a way to stop my wig obeying the laws of gravity, I went over the lyrics to 'When You're Good to Mama', and started thinking about my own. *If she found out about tonight, she'd be so ashamed of me … whatever I do, there's no way she or Dad can know about this.* I started to take in the crumbling brown walls of the mouldy crypt, the condensation coating its ceiling, and the general mess and chaos around me. I felt an intense pang of anguish, as if a capsule of sorrow had suddenly dissolved in my gut and was spreading rapidly around my bloodstream. I couldn't help but equate the filth of the room with the image my mother had of me – a skinny, broke Arab son in a dress, wheezing because of the disgusting room they now found themselves in. It was as though the dirt of the surroundings was a mirror to the person I really was, and I sat immobilised, unable to do anything, locked in a limbo of heartache.

Soon though, one of the other queens saw me sitting in stasis with the doors about to open at any moment. In a silent act of solidarity, they made up my face. This was the first instance of the powerful sisterhood I have come to find in the drag community. On later getting to know this person, I discovered that they had lost their father as a baby, and also struggled with feelings of familial dislocation. In that moment, both of us were grieving and being restored.

Before I could fully tumble down this well of sadness, the first guests arrived, and I ran to the bathroom to firmly place a lid on it. Seeing my reflection in drag for the very first time was an uncanny kind of reunion, an introduction to a person I had always had inside me, yet had somehow always missed. I recognised the person in the mirror more than I had ever recognised my own image, experiencing the same fuzzy harmony as when I first gazed into a formless marine aquarium. Again, my gender dysphoria was suddenly appeased, and here in front of me was a true manifestation of my internal self. It was time for everyone to meet her.

It was moving to see so many students come to support the evening, most of whom attended in some kind of drag. As soon as there was an audience, I interacted with them as my drag character Glamrou, an overly confident and acerbic queen who says the things that nobody else dares to. As people took their seats – i.e. the floor of a low-ceilinged cave – I lap-danced those who were willing, with the sexual litheness of a lemur and the confidence of a peacock.

One of the things that I've come to find interesting about being in drag is that once you're dressed and made up, you so rarely *see* yourself in drag (unless your outfit involves some kind of reflective device). As a result, your image belongs more to the people who are viewing you, and you start to perceive yourself in how you are being perceived in the eyes gazing at you. That night, the eyes of everyone I spoke to seemed bewitched by the confidence of the queen in their presence, with no knowledge of the sorrowing mess she had been just moments before the doors opened. By the time it came to perform my number, I tried to summon the matriarchal majesty of Queen Latifah in the *Chicago* ballad, and my performance, though unquestionably a hot mess, incorporated numerous thigh slaps, grinding of audience members, and a power that I didn't even know I had. There was a person in the front row whose mouth was on the floor as they stared up at me, and afterwards they remarked that they'd never seen 'femininity' so unreservedly celebrated before.

After the final number – one of the queens singing an aching rendition of 'I Am What I Am' – I thanked the crowd for coming to support us, and whipped out a set of queer platitudes you'd find in any gay anthem: 'Remember to be yourself', 'You're all superstars', and a direct bit of plagiarism, 'You were born this way!' After that, Lady Gaga's empowering queer anthem blasted through the room, every single person stood up, and we danced in what was one of the biggest emotional releases of my life. One of the queens who I still perform with, Shirley Du Naughty, ran up to me, and we hugged tightly. The evening was a beautiful celebration of so much. It went on late into the night, and I can still feel every single beat of it.

When I finally got to my room at about five in the morning, the intense triumph of the evening slowly dissipated, and, as the wig came off, the shame slid over me to replace it. I stared at my reflection. I looked like a genderless newt whose face had melted, and the starkness of my bare-walled college room made me feel terrifyingly lonely. I took a sleeping pill and didn't wake until 3 p.m. the next day.

Whenever I woke up in my university dorms, the first thing I experienced was panic, and this became attached to anxieties surrounding my phone. *Will there be a series of missed calls or prosecuting text messages from my parents? Will I have been found out somehow? Has someone at Cambridge discovered that my 'celebrate all of who you are' mottos are utterly phoney? Or has someone in my family got wind of my drag night? Which side of myself has been ousted by another side?* And so the morning after the first Denim, panic woke me from my slumber, and I grabbed my phone, scrolling past the numerous messages of praise and gratitude from students to see if there was anything reprimanding from my parents. I was terrified they'd got wind of the evening all the way from Dubai. After a manic scroll, I realised that for now, I was in the clear.

But this, in essence, was the experience of my early drag career. Something at once so liberating soon became a second closet, both literally and metaphorically, full of sequins, patent leather heels and glittery eyeshadow, but also secrets, both magical and shameful.

The buzz I felt from Glamrou's first outing was unlike anything else, and even knowing all the problems this would probably throw my way, I needed to experience it again. For so long my male body had been judged a failure, physically, socially, sexually and religiously, and now, as my female alter ego, I had agency and strength. While in the past femininity had brought with it a whole panoply of issues – both at home and at school – in drag, femininity became armour, and the more of it I flaunted, the more powerful I became. This was not something I could ever turn away from. And so I continued drag throughout my time as a student, and the events got bigger and bigger.

One of the major events was an 800-strong party at the historic Cambridge Union. We decorated the venue first by placing acetate over the portraits of stuffy white masters and giving them all 'lipstick' with coloured markers. So far, so good. But I think that was one of the only things that didn't go wrong that night. Most of it was a disaster of farcical proportions.

The ticket to the party was meant to be a neon pink wristband reading DENIM; the idea was that when instructed, the crowd would raise their arms to create an anemone of UV-light. On the day the wristbands were due to arrive I woke up at 6 a.m., rushing with excitement at the thought of turning the brown-panelled Union walls pink. I cycled to the Union to check them out, my prized red billowing cape getting stuck in the wheels as it did every day, and skipped to the front office, almost mounting the huge parcel that lay there with my name on it. I tore open the box, and grabbed a wristband. There it was – a popping neon pink. And on the front? It said DEMIN. *Maybe it's a mistake.* I dived back in, hoping that this was a singular freak accident. DEMIN. *Third time lucky?* DEMIN. All 800 of them said DEMIN. D-E-M-I-N. With the profound sadness of a kid who doesn't get the video game they dreamt of at Christmas, I met up with the producer I worked with at the time. She lit her third cigarette in a row and smoked the whole thing in silence. Then she said, 'I've got it! How about we change the tagline of the event to *GET DEM-IN DENIM*.' At this moment, I cried.

Perhaps the 'DEMIN-DENIM-saga' was a bad omen, because from there the catastrophes multiplied. The Union was not actually equipped to throw a concert for 800 students, and so the sound system was grossly inadequate for the space. Of course, we only found this out during the opening number. In my bedroom I had come up with a remix of Lady Gaga's 'Bad Romance' and Madonna's 'Vogue' – yes, I was what you might call 'a basic gay' – which was entirely choreographed for the floor with us five queens singing on Britney-style radio mics. The mics, however, did not work. Did we know this? No. Not till after the song. And how long was the song? Seven minutes. Does it get worse? Of course it does. The stage we hired was built so low that only the front row could actually see any of the floor-work choreography we'd worked on day and night for months. The vast majority of the 800 students who stood behind them could only see the tops of our wigs. So for seven minutes almost 750 people watched the tips of five wigs bobbing up and down to absolutely no music.

The failure of the show felt emotionally cataclysmic. The fact that I had failed within a queer space was like a double punch, as if the sin-collecting angel had shown up again, saying, 'You deserved to fail for being so sinful.' Drag, for the most part, felt like it could exist on a different plateau of reality to the one I failed in on the outside world, and although an ephemeral space, it was one where I could at least pretend to be victorious. Any kind of failure within a safe queer space that I'd constructed felt like a colossal GAME OVER. After the show of five-wigs-no-sound ended, the rest of Denim partied away into the night, and I retreated to the balcony, watching on as hundreds of students danced free from gender norms. From my seat in the gods, I wanted to feel happy that I'd been able to orchestrate this happening, but instead I felt devastated at its ephemeral fragility; I knew that as soon as the DJ ended their set, I'd have to get home and take off my drag, and any sense of invincibility would be immediately obliterated. Looking down at the intertwining mass of optimistic student queerness, I didn't feel hopeful that such a space could exist – I was saddened by its transience. As with my aquarium, I was once again gazing at a queer wonderland, but couldn't find a way in.

Even though drag brought with it its own set of disappointments, the feelings of empowerment it brought me were still too significant to ignore. When I was a teenager, my social self was founded upon erasing or exaggerating narratives of my life. In drag, I felt as if I was performatively rewriting those narratives.

Drag is a visual assertion of identity that doesn't rely on words or explanations. When you walk into a room in drag, you immediately take up space. Your stilettoes echo and your fabrics billow; the glitter on your eyelids refracts the light, and your every step has heft. When I teach on drag courses to those early in their drag career, this is one of the first things I work on with students – I tell them to be 'moved' by their own presence, to treat every step they take into a room as a cinematic event. I want them to be so consumed by the sheer profundity of their existence that they move themselves to tears with every motion. A drag queen whose work has been of immeasurable inspiration to me, Victoria Sin, taught me a lot about this. When they are in drag, they move at a gloriously laconic pace, and talk at half the speed of regular conversation, confronting everyone in the room with their sumptuous presence, and on their own terms.

When I created Glamrou, my drag persona, I replaced my long-felt invisibility with ultra visibility, and it told the world that I loved being me. It told the world that I was proud to be queer. It told the world that I was defiantly myself. As Glamrou, I got to live out thought patterns that were the opposite of those that governed the entirety of my day out of drag. I saw this too in the rest of my Denim queens. There was one who, out of drag, was always uncommonly polite and so sweet-natured; in drag, his character was a monstrous murderer. One of the other queens struggled with body image issues, and anxieties about their sexual attractiveness to other men – in drag, they were unapologetically sexy, body positive, and seductive. Drag is like a form of hypnotherapy; in your drag persona, you mute the engrained cognitive patterns to create new, positive neurological pathways. The more and more your drag character evolves, the more these affirmations become part of yourself out of drag. Not that I'm saying the murderous queen became a murderer out of drag, but over the course of their drag career, it's been moving to see the confidence it has given him to assert his opinion when necessary, and to abstain from apologising when not necessary.

My experience, however, was that the more Glamrou got to experience the things I wished I really felt myself, the more Amrou felt deprived of those privileges. And that's partly because the more Glamrou succeeded as a drag queen, the more Amrou suffered in real life. The worst of it came during a summer show Denim did in a West End theatre in London. It was only a one-night event, but it was an extremely exciting moment for us to be able to take our drag to a prominent London stage, and we were all really excited. Each of the other Denims had their family in to watch the show, and I always found this difficult. At this point in my life my parents lived in the Middle East, and I shared absolutely zero details of my life with them. Least of all about Denim. The only real links to my family I had were Majid and Lily (my father's old friend and his girlfriend). I grew particularly close with Lily over this period – she was someone I could speak to about my sexuality, and pretty much all her friends were gay. Majid knew my father, so I had to be careful of what I said around him – but he also partied *religiously* in Mykonos (the decadent Greek island), and he was an example to me of an Arab breaking the rules. I loved Lily, and I wanted to love Majid so that I could have a connection with someone close to my father who might in some way understand me. Every so often, he suggested that he did, like the night he drunkenly texted me a video of some drag queens in Barcelona he was watching. But, notwithstanding his 'against-the-Iraqi mould' activities, as a wealthy and unreserved patriarch, he was still a very respected figure in our community.

Feeling hopeful, I invited Majid and Lily to the show – it was playing with fire, but I needed Amrou's and Glamrou's worlds to collide, to feel as if they were working in harmony, not in fractured opposition. Majid ignored my message – I assumed he was silently proud, only ignoring me to save face in the community – and Lily said she'd come with her gay cohort. Throughout the show, I felt tidal waves of support coming from her eyes; she was no longer looking at the floor as she had during the Macaulay Culkin episode, but instead looked up at me proudly, having known since I was a kid that this was a part of me that I needed to express. In the dressing room after the show, it was one of the first times I didn't feel weighed down with post-show sorrow – because I had some semblance of family out there.

I got to be like the other queens, packing away their drag in the comfort that their family would be out there telling them they were proud.

But as I waltzed into the bar, ready to experience a familial embrace, Lily was nowhere to be found. I looked everywhere for her, and theorised that she might be having a late-night dinner somewhere. I called and texted her, and eventually she messaged with 'I had to go home. Well done baby.' For Lily, this was cold. I had half expected her to be wailing in tears and telling me that it was the proudest she'd ever been in her life. This message felt perfunctory, even clinical. And it was unlike her. But as it turns out, Majid had seen a photo of me performing that night (Lily's friend had uploaded it onto Facebook straight after the show). He called her home to berate her, and next he would come for me. The following morning, after I was woken by my everyday surge of panic, my hand swiping my phone to check for any notifications of potential life catastrophes, there it finally was: an emotional grenade in the guise of an email from my father's oldest friend Majid. It went something like this:

Your dad made constant sacrifices so he could give you a good life. And you're repaying him how? With this drag nonsense that is bringing your family nothing but shame. Until you stop your selfish stupidity, I want nothing more to do with you. Do not contact me until you've finally grown up.

I read it three times in a row. The first time I processed only the shape of the words, scanning the emotionally abusive message with the coldness of a forensic specialist. On the second read, I consumed every word very slowly. Each one was like a blade slicing through my insides. The third time, I read it even more slowly, scouring it for any potential subtext that might negate the cruelty of the message. No such luck. I immediately got out of bed, took my phone, and left the house. It was a hot summer's day, and I lay on the grass in the nearby park for hours, willing the sun to incinerate me until I was nothing but ash.

Majid, who I had come to believe was a true renegade ally, once told me that his own lifestyle did not need such policing because of one key distinction: for the most part, he did it in private. His constant partying in Mykonos and his almost comical disregard for Islam were never called into question, because in public Arab spaces, he presented as a rich, conformist and culturally observant man, like a KGB spy undercover in America. Drag, however, immediately makes visible what no one is ready to acknowledge. It disrupts boundaries between the private and public, and visibly tells the people around you that you are different and not afraid to show it.

There are many Muslims and Arab cousins of mine who similarly defy the gender codes of our community – but they are able to save face in public. Collective responsibility is a huge pressure; your parents impress upon you the need to uphold a set of behaviours and principles because they too had to sacrifice their identities to these structures; the delicate house of mirrors is kept stable because of the silent assumption that everyone in the room will play along and keep the fantasy alive. I have seen female cousins of mine out in nightclubs high on drugs with tattoos all over their backs, and then seen them performing the role of modest Arab daughter at functions the next day. I have seen my parents once nearly hitting each other in a fight at home, only then to embody the image of total domestic bliss soon afterwards at a cousin's birthday. Paradoxically, for me to perform in an identity so unashamedly 'artificial' was a threat to a man who believed the health of the community depended on an unacknowledged artificiality. He didn't stop at the email. Wanting to scare me out of drag for good, he sent the incriminating photo of me onstage to my parents. (This was of me in hot pants grinding with the floor and pretending that the microphone was a penis). *Cheers, Majid.*

As it was the university holidays, my parents were visiting me in London (they did this every summer that I was a student). When I went to visit them, entering the house felt like enrolling in an army school for disobedient children. I walked in, and tried to watch the TV – the remote was snatched from me, and the TV was turned off. My father, now completely white in the hair and aged in the face, didn't look me in the eye. My mother's eyes were puffy from crying. They retreated to their room. I went into mine and decided to change into something more comfortable.

When I opened my wardrobe, my favourite red cape was nowhere to be seen. Soon, I realised – none of my clothes were. Everything with a trace of flamboyance was missing. Feeling as if a limb had been cut off, I had to ask my parents where my clothes from Cambridge had suddenly disappeared to. 'We threw away all your silly clothes, Amrou. Enough is enough,' my mother said, more sorrow in her voice than anything malicious, as if she were a pet owner announcing that they had to put down a dog that they loved. 'It's time for you to act like a man.' Having my prized garments tossed away felt like an act of castration – these were all I had to express my queer identity, and each and every one of them had gone. The red cape had become a staple piece of mine at Cambridge, and there was even a month when I wore it with red boots, red trousers and dyed my hair bright red. I similarly did this with a green ensemble, effectively treating the separate academic terms as if I was a different fruit in a Pimm's drink each time. The immediate concern was superficial – *what Pimm's fruit am I going to impersonate at Cambridge now?!* – but beneath that was a deep pain and a feeling of having been neutered.

The atmosphere in the house was that of a 1920s psychiatric ward. I felt as if I were being forcibly medicated, so that I would emerge a son of whom they were proud. My parents scheduled a family meeting for the end of the week, which I anticipated would be the final assessment of whether the week's treatment had been curative. It seemed that they had both rehearsed the conversation – my mother even had bullet points to guide her through it (on a pink heart-shaped Post-it, no less). The psychological takedown went something like this (imagine the following text being uttered by either one of them, as it was clearly a rehearsed script written by them both):

'Amrou. You used to be a very special, happy kid.' *Yes, and I miss that time.*

'You were our pride and joy.' *Let me guess, I'm not any more?*

'But you've become a monster.' *Nope, definitely not.*

'Ever since coming to the UK, look what happened to you.' *So we're blaming this on Britain?*

'You've become angry, rude, selfish.' *Angry – I can't help it. Rude ... you deserve it. But selfish?*

'How am I selfish?' I asked, completely sincerely.

'All you do is what you want. You dress how you want, do what you want, act how you want, and you don't care that it makes us upset. That is the definition of selfish.' *Not in the Oxford English Dictionary, Mother.*

'But ... I'm just trying to do what makes me happy ... it's not about *you*. It's about me.'

'You see – that's selfish. You're selfish.' *Damn. They got me on semantics.*

'I'm just trying to be me.'

'You're not you. Everything you do is a reflection of us. And with all this women's clothing nonsense you have lost the respect of Majid' – *who parties with drag queens in Barcelona?* – 'and you have made life hell for us. People in

Iraq message us with photos of you. It's bad for business, and it's bad for the family. Have you no shame?'

'I don't mean for that to happen! I'm just trying to be me! What's selfish is you throwing out all my clothes because you don't want me to be gay. That's you only thinking about you.'

'Amrou,' my mother said, in a cat-purring whisper that she knew would tug at my heartstrings. 'You used to make me so happy. Now, everything that you do … it makes me unhappy. You are the source of my life's unhappiness.' *I hate that you think I'm responsible for all your hurt. I'm so sorry you're hurt.* 'The things that you do … this gay stuff … these dresses. They make me unhappy. So if you want me to be happy, stop them, and all will be well. OK?'

My mother and father were both crying, and it was clear how genuinely they felt what they were saying. As I stared at them, the two people who made me exist but made me want to not exist, the two people who created me but were ashamed of their creation – their queer Frankenstein's monster – I experienced a sharp duality of emotion. I felt rage and venom that my protectors wanted to hurt the part of me that was really me, but guilt and grief that I had upset two people who had done so much for me. It was hard not to feel remorse. With hindsight I understand how unfair it was of them to place the wealth of their life's unhappiness onto me, a person only trying to express themselves, but within the very specific context of our family and cultural heritage, I was the person doing the upsetting. Also, they had strength in numbers and the community, with decades of a tried and tested formula to back them up; I had only a very feeble sense of what I was trying to do. 'I'm sorry,' I said, half meaning it, half not.

'Amrou. You seem so … confused about your life. What do you really want?' I sat with this question for a long moment, intending to answer it genuinely. 'I just want to be with someone and for them to love me.'

Of course they both knew that this 'someone' I referred to wouldn't be a future wife, and after they searched for something to say, my mother came out with: 'It would be unfair for you to inflict yourself on somebody. You're impossible to love.' I already fully believed this, but that didn't make hearing it any less devastating.

When I went back to Cambridge for the start of my third year, drag seemed the only way to numb the pain of that brutal familial blow-up – moments in drag made me feel, on even just a superficial level, worthy of love (which I equated only with applause). But it was also the drag that was worsening the dynamic in my family – was it an unsustainable high that made the lows of my life more intense? Drag felt like a glittery Hello Kitty plaster covering up an oozing wound of rejection beneath, and whenever I ripped it off, the wound grew more infected. There was, as a result, a marked contradiction between my external and internal selves. And this led to some surprising and often saddening behaviours.

*

During my time at Cambridge, I had become close friends with the most wondrous of boys. Let's call him Dennis. I first met Dennis out at a nightclub called Cindy's, which was notorious for having a floor so sticky that you could barely move your feet, and usually hosted the inebriated conclusions of most sporting society escapades. It was shit.

During my first term, I went with my college drinking society – the college I studied at is called Corpus Christi, and the drinking society was called the Corpus Cossacks. AWFUL. I spent most of the night in the smoking area, hopping from person to person in the hope that one might socially adopt me. As I leant against a wall to smoke a cigarette, trying desperately to imitate James Dean but probably coming across more like a meerkat, I caught sight of a beautiful cherubic boy, with huge, spellbinding eyes that could swallow a galaxy, staring through the crowd at me with a coy, nervous smile. He walked over. 'I'm Dennis … we have a couple of mutual friends in London. I've been wanting to say hey for ages.' I cannot express to you how utterly enchanting this boy was. He was like the human manifestation of Puck from *A Midsummer Night's Dream*, with the infectiously mischievous grin of, well, Dennis the Menace. At this point in his life, Dennis hadn't come out of the closet, but I could immediately recognise a queer spirit that gave us an affinity.

The intensity of the bond Dennis and I shared brought with it an entire world of secret idioms that only we were privy to, and this feeling of coexisting with someone else on a planet out of orbit from everybody else's was very special. We developed a reputation as a bit of a double act, and I adored this sense of social solidarity we had. Things really cemented when we went on a European drama society tour together. Dennis and I were both performers, and stupidly signed ourselves up to the university's infamous winter tour of a Shakespeare production around European high schools. In essence, the tour consisted of travelling through ice-cold snow to put on a pathetic production of *The Taming of the Shrew* to schools that had no interest in watching us, and it was quite, quite, miserable. Dennis and I quickly formed an alliance in our misery, and created our own queer sub-culture. While the majority of the cast attempted to enjoy what is genuinely one of the worst shows I have ever been involved in, Dennis and I decided to camp the fuck out of it, which made performing in the stale production actually quite joyous. During a day off, when the cast rented a chalet and built a snowman as a bonding exercise, Dennis and I decided instead to ski on a nearby slope in just jeans and gilets. During the daily installation and dismantling of the set, where the cast were forced to carry a *helter skelter* through blizzards, magical Dennis and I would do photoshoots in the snow and pretend to be on a runway as we carried the metal structure, which was so cold that it fused with our fingers. We had developed such a well-constructed reputation for being 'cast divas' – as if this is an insult! – that we decided to fulfil everyone's expectations of us by flying back to the UK instead of enduring the coach ride with everybody else. While the debris of the production was being lugged back into the truck, the cast members looked on in disdain as Dennis and I wheeled our bags through the snow to a waiting cab, both with pink pashminas billowing in the blizzard, victoriously cheeky smiles on our faces.

Dennis identified as heterosexual in the first year of our friendship, but it was clear how much he looked up to me for being out as gay. I recognised so much of myself in him; how his queer spirit fully took flight when he was on the stage, his anxieties at having upset people or about being found out over absolutely anything, and an at times crippling OCD that really hindered his quality of life. His OCD took a much more poetic form than mine, though; for instance, when I once directed him in a theatre production, he had to watch a scene from *Black Beauty* every single night before he could get onstage. I was acutely aware of how much was holding him back, and wanted no more than to see him flourish. It became a mission of mine to watch this angel properly spread his wings, and casting him as the lead of a production I directed was a particularly powerful moment. Every night, as he hypnotised the room with his completely unique flair – not a gecko costume in sight – I felt deeply proud of him. But I also felt as if I was watching a manifestation of my child self, and my protective instinct over Dennis was almost as if I were trying to save a version of myself from the onslaught of emotional trauma that I knew was coming.

The night Dennis came out to me, we had just been to a debate between the Cambridge Footlights and the cast from *Made in Chelsea*, the motion being: 'I'd rather be in Cambridge than in Chelsea'. It wasn't at all compelling (nor all that funny). As my beautiful red cape had been taken from me, I was wearing a new velvet black one, which everyone knew was just not as good; I had searched from vintage shop to vintage shop, attempting to find something similar, and this was the best I could muster. After the 'debate' finished, I ran cape-first out of the hall, and Dennis asked if he could speak to me. With my cape acting as a sort of shared picnic blanket, Dennis sat opposite me, full of hope and pride in his eyes. 'Amrou, I have something to tell you,' he said, clearly anticipating the significance of this moment, a life milestone he had probably imagined countless times. Before he had a chance to tell me himself, I came out with, 'Are you gay, Dennis?' He had the disappointed expression of someone having their own anecdote interrupted at a dinner party. 'Oh ... well ... yeah,' said Dennis. Given how close we were, and how much my externally strong queer identity had done for us both, I think he expected me to lift him up with a sisterly pride. In truth, I had anticipated this kind of reaction for myself too. But all I felt was rage. It was like an allergic reaction. His eyes, which just a moment ago had glowed with hopeful electricity, suddenly dimmed as he registered my coldness. 'Oh, cool,' I said, breathing quietly to resist whatever it was that seemed to want to come out of me. I think what was upsetting me the most was the sheer honesty of his coming out. Nothing was forced … it felt completely authentic. And I was unnerved by the way that he did it, as if I were a queer leader who had won over another recruit. How could I tell him I was proud of him for coming out when I could only feel shame for my own sexuality? Surely a flamboyant, public drag queen would feel nothing but warmth and joy for their best friend finding the courage to come out in some part through their friendship? Instead I felt bitter that my queer positivity could help someone else find happiness when that very same queer positivity was ripping me ever further from my family.

I was a very bad friend during Dennis's coming out. It is another one of the things I'm ashamed of most in my life, the fact that I couldn't be a pillar of support and pride for this extraordinary boy who had finally found his voice. He wanted to talk to me about every step of his journey, and each and every moment became a reflection of how unresolved I was on the inside. Every now and then we would see each other, and as he told me about his parents' reaction to his sexuality, and their promise of unconditional support to him, I couldn't even muster a smile. Even though I wore ostentatious clothes, dressed in drag, and roamed the university as if I were trying to convert everyone to homosexuality, the growing acceptance Dennis had for himself and from his family only highlighted how constructed my façade was, and how little I really had. The more at ease he became with himself, a fluid, queer person swimming smoothly through the streets, the more I felt like a badly put together puppet in comparison, all the seams starting to tear. I began to avoid him. He had expressed interest in wanting to go out to gay clubs with me, but whenever the weekly LGBT night was on, I ignored his calls. It broke my heart to do this, but it felt essential. My queer identity was something that I had cultivated as a mask; I believed somehow, that my professed queer identity was the only thing that stopped me feeling the decay inside me. I needed to protect the night as something that was definitively mine; I just couldn't share it with Dennis, even though he had just as much of a right to it as I did.

When Dennis began exploring sex, I grew even more jealous. He showed me pictures of all the gorgeous boys that he was experimenting with, and, instead of celebrating the pursuit of his desires, I reflected on Mason, and how my sexual history revolved around feelings of worthlessness and punishment. The more empowered Dennis became in his own desirability, the more grotesque I felt by comparison. *How is it that he can come out and find so much freedom and validation in his sexuality?* Even though I inhabited a drag persona that would suggest I too had freedom and validation, it certainly wasn't like that for me. My sexual episodes with Mason, along with the fact that I had been equating homosexuality with an eternity in hell for so long, meant that sex was like going on a rollercoaster without a safety belt. As a student, I found it difficult to believe that anybody attractive could actually desire me. Glamrou, on the contrary, was the ultimate seductress – indeed, she *performed* the role of sexual empowerment, but never actualised it. *How is it that Dennis has found so much empowerment with sex, and I have none?*

The relationship between drag and sex is complicated. In drag, you have an innate confidence, and this to others comes across as sexy. You can inhabit tropes and ideas of sexiness, but it is a performance. Nevertheless, this doesn't stop people from touching you without being invited, as if your inhabited sexiness must mean you'll be up for anything. Mostly, in drag, I feel utterly asexual, even though I present as highly sexual. A lot of this is down to pure practicality. My penis, for a start, lives taped away between my butt cheeks (essentially, I'm fucking myself). The amount of paint on my face and the sheer heaviness of the fabric and ornaments is also a lot of strain on the body – it's like being corseted by an image of sexiness. None of this is helped by the fact that gay men have a very odd relationship with drag queens. For the most part, they celebrate and whoop for drag queens, but want little to do with them sexually – like we're there to be enjoyed as abstract entities of queerness, but not as literal, sexual people.

Many gay men, on finding out I do drag, are turned off. 'But I'm into guys,' is something I've heard before, or, as one total bonehead I spoke to said, 'I only date manly men.' This deification of masculinity in the gay community is an endemic issue that deserves its own book to dismantle, but one of the reasons it's so pervasive is because a lot of gay men, who have endured or fear familial and social rejections, want no more reminders of their 'nonconformism'. It's why body fascism exists so deeply in gay male spaces – the crisis of masculinity that comes from being gay can sometimes manifest in a vigorous over-compensation. So while drag itself was utterly empowering, it made my desirability among gay men dwindle. I was once rejected from a *gay* club in London for being too feminine, and when I first started drag, I would always make sure to hide my glittery costumes in the closet and scratch off any remaining nail polish for when dates came over. While Dennis embodied and felt his sexiness, becoming truly confident as a queer, sexual male, my drag paradoxically robbed me of this.

When Dennis found intimacy and started having relationships, I felt as if I really was nothing by comparison. Within the year of his coming out, he won the support of his parents and found the joys of sex. While I held my mother's belief that 'it would be unfair to inflict myself on anyone', here Dennis was, able to negotiate intimacy as if it weren't some unpredictable home-made bomb device. This was something I had no clue how to do. The idea of being emotionally intimate with somebody felt as alien to me as sci-fi. *How do people do this? Do these people just share the things about themselves and get love in return? Surely that's an impossibility? Intimacy must be some kind of hoax.*

Even my body rejected intimacy as if it were a virus. As a student, I developed a sexual reflex that was completely out of my control: I covered my face every time I ejaculated during intercourse. Whenever I felt the surge of an orgasmic release, both hands – or whichever was available – would come up to prevent my coming face from public view. Moments of ejaculation have often involved little control for me. I used to suffer hugely from premature ejaculation, as if my brain was telling my body I wasn't allowed to be having gay sex. The moment of ejaculation is when your identity dissolves temporarily, and this lack of control over how I was being perceived seemed to instruct my nervous system to shield my face. I had learnt to be equipped with my armours of identity – from colourful clothes and gaudy jewellery to well-rehearsed anecdotes and witty turns of phrase – so that when I was without them, like during sex, my brain instinctually went into the defensive. All sexual partners I had expressed their frustration over this tic of mine. 'I want to feel connected with you when you come.' *I can't let you see the real me – trust me, you don't want to.*

The only person who could have possibly been my boyfriend was a boy at Cambridge who helped produce Denim in its second year. He was a lovely, handsome, big-hearted guy, who showed me only kindness. I adored him. Let's call him Felix. The first time we kissed was in my first year, at the end of a May Ball. These are the black-tie parties that colleges throw; they're hideously indulgent and drenched in gallons of champagne. Of course, ever the hypocrite, I went to as many as I could. If you could block out the almost sickening privilege on show, and how grossly indicative it was of the inequality of British social structures – an inequality in which I was clearly complicit – the setting was absurdly romantic.

It was 6 a.m., the sun had risen, and we stood on a bridge overlooking a river of punts teeming with passed-out students in their finery. Before us were the expansive lawns, the dew just starting to rise. We bumped into each other for the first time that night, and as I was a little high on drugs, we kissed. This became an electrifying fit of passion, our tongues and arms enveloping each other like intertwining snakes. We ran off to a park with some of his friends, and cuddled until the early afternoon.

Soon afterwards, we met up, and had a wonderful date, comparing notes on our fears of familial rejection and the struggles of coming out. One night during the university break, I went clubbing with him and his friends in London, and was delighted to see him. Felix was a very attentive date that evening, showing me affection, and letting the entire club know that he was proud to be with me. I wanted to go with it, but the more affection he showed me, the more nervous I felt, and the more he tried, the more my body physically resisted, even though my desires were pulling me towards him. I was sweating profusely, and became light-headed, and had to excuse myself. Outside, in the pouring rain, I suffered a panic attack, and had to get in a cab home, where I took a sleeping pill to neutralise my angst. I ignored Felix for the better part of a year, and I hated myself for it, but it felt like the most natural thing to do.

At a graduation party in a friend's house a year and a bit later, Felix, emotionally riled up, confronted me in the corner. 'I've just found out I have six months to live,' he said, stern and matter-of-fact. I completely freaked out, and was emotionally beside myself, before he said, 'I'm not ill. That was a lie.'

'Why the fuck would you do that to me? I was so upset … that really hurt,' I screamed at him, shaken.

'Well you hurt *me* pretty bad. Actually, what you did really fucked me up.' And then Felix left. We were both high, which might explain his decision to test me in such a brutal fashion, but it's clear he was punishing me for my sudden silence and erasing of our relationship. What I did was undeniably cruel, but it was hard to explain that I didn't have any control over it. My body quite simply wouldn't allow me to pursue the direction of my desires – they were working against each other, as if I were a medieval torture victim whose limbs were being pulled in opposite directions. This relationship timeline was replicated with three other boys while I was at Cambridge; I felt an instinctive urge to flee after the third date, and I was powerless to stop it. This was the summation of my romantic life as a 'proud queer person', and being around Dennis painfully highlighted this. Dennis and I drifted apart in my final year, and the loss of our friendship hit me hard.

I cared a great deal about the queer community, and had sacrificed so much to set up safe spaces for students to explore their gender and sexual identity in an open way. I would have done anything to keep my drag sisters safe, and worked tirelessly to make my identity political. So, on a personal level, how could I treat these wonderful gay men, the beautiful Dennis and the lovely Felix, my emotional allies, in the way that I did? It's devastating, really, how awful queer people can be to other queer people, when what they're really trying to fight are the wider social structures attacking their queerness. We enact repeated cycles of rejection upon each other, obliterating ourselves like aimless Pac-Mans circling a doomed maze.

My early experiences in drag, as much as they were empowering, also felt like dissociative episodes, as though my various selves were splitting into multiple, separate manifestations. I could not figure out how the fuck to merge them together, although with hindsight, the solutions are more obvious. For starters – I was only dressing as white women.

Recently, on that kind of Saturday night when a lack of plans turns to a narcissistic scrolling through every picture ever taken of you on Facebook, I realised, four hours into the void of urban loneliness, that my drag was only referencing Western images of femininity. All my looks were inspired by some image of Western celebrity I had admired. I owned wigs in the style of Lady Gaga, 80s blazers in the vein of (a very unpolished) Madonna, and pretty much everything else was an iteration of Carrie Bradshaw. My early drag was the continuation of me trying to wear the costume of the West at Eton, albeit in a very different guise. In the first five years of performing at drag shows, I did not once address my race. It had zero impact on my material, and I think I was trying to escape all the structures of my race and heritage that I held responsible for my pain. I thought that my drag was a form of 'Western liberation', and many commented that I was a particularly 'wild' performer. There was one show where I wore just knickers and a wig – without realising that a *hanger* was caught in it – and spent most of the set thrusting against the floor and moaning, in what must have seemed like a sorry mix between an improvised dance class and an exorcism. In drag, I would get absurdly drunk, mount people uninvited – if you are a survivor of this, *I'M SORRY* – and would often end up half naked on a pole screaming 'I'M FREE MUTHAFUCKAS', like that annoying person at a party who asks everyone to watch them dance when the chorus comes in (and it doesn't for quite some time). During sets, I became a mascot for secularism, shouting 'FUCK RELIGION' and 'FIGHT THE SYSTEM!' I mixed up all the problematic Western platitudes that I felt had given me a voice. Drag spliced me from myself, my past, and the parts of me that I had completely fallen out of touch with.

One summer while I was at Cambridge, we were invited to play at the 500th anniversary ball of St John's College. It would be Denim's largest performance so far. We had a set in the historic halls, singing and dancing in drag in a brown panelled time-warp that reeked of historical privilege. It's hard to walk around Cambridge and not feel seduced by the vaulted cloisters and the Gothic spires – the grandeur immediately tells you that the place is worth something, and it's difficult to fight the impulse to want to be accepted within it. It's also hard to ignore the fact that pretty much every single portrait hanging in pretty much every single college is of a white man in black robes. When I see such exclusion, there is an inherent drive in me to try to find a place within the very institution that seems to be excluding me. So how seductive it was indeed to be invited to perform in an institution so steeped in opulence and lineage, and *in drag* too. It felt as if the child Amrou who wanted nothing more than parental acceptance was now being accepted by the arms of a different kind of conservative institution, and one much more majestic. *If I can be accepted as queer by an institution that might usually reject me – then I'm no longer worthless.*

I became addicted to gigs like the ones at St John's. I wanted to find the straightest crowds, the most patriarchal of audiences, the most archaic of milieus, and win their love, all in the hope that I might no longer feel like someone abandoned by the first institution we're all born into – family. It was almost as if I was trying to be a Trojan Horse, smuggling myself into the barriered room, not only planning to ransack it, but be accepted within it.

I experience this same instinct whenever I go to straight weddings. As I pan around to watch all the married couples with their children, and the traditional romantic ceremony that tells your friends and family that you've succeeded in finding love, I feel simultaneously an urge to reject the weary heteronormativity of the entire proceedings, and a desperation to be part of it. In an early Denim show, I wore a white bridal gown while singing Gaga's 'Marry the Night', in an attempt to assert my right to a place in this white ceremonial tradition (but on queer terms). I was desperate to present as transgressive, but also to be entirely accepted within spaces that were anything but that. This conflict meant that being in drag during those early days always felt combative, and rooted in conflict. I was accustomed to thinking of myself as someone inherently transgressive because of the way that I was raised; all initial experiences in drag hence felt like a performance of the belief that my existence was by nature hostile. I wanted this hostility to be accepted by institutions that might otherwise not want me. Perhaps this is why I always dressed as white women – *accept my queerness, and I'll accept your whiteness.*

This desire to lie in bed with the establishment started taking very literal form in my sexual fetish for white, partnered, heterosexual men. After my brief flirtations with genuine intimacy, gay men started to terrify me. If I was at a party, say, and I hit it off with an attractive man, I'd hope upon hope that they were straight. For if that were the case, then I wouldn't have to worry about my possibly being rejected by them in any real way, or face the risk of some gut-churning intimacy. As soon as I learnt that the boundary of heterosexuality stood in the way, my desires could be expressed according to a pattern I recognised. Eventually, sexually experimenting with men who identified as heterosexual became the only way I ever had sex. But as much as I was drawn to these men, it felt like they were seeking me out too. Without even making a conscious decision, a night out dancing would usually end in me kissing a man who later told me he had a wife or girlfriend. The mere glint in their eye let me know that they were a sexually curious 'straight man' who felt like they could have something from me. After one of these nights, which ended in me giving the guy a hand job in an alleyway in Soho, I asked the man what it was that made him desire me.

'I dunno … you just seem so … confident … sexually free.' *LOL. But I guess the charade is working.*

'You make being gay seem … so … fun.' *It's hellish too, hun.*

'I wanted to, you know … have a go.' *So I'm your guinea pig?*

There was something that turned me on about being viewed as this kind of sexual experiment. It immediately resonated with me because it made my identity feel like something taboo, and this was a natural place for me to occupy psychologically. If I could win around these men, then maybe I could win around the two people who also felt that they couldn't love me as I am because it was against the rules – my parents.

This was especially the case with one man (a doctor who we'll call Joseph). Joseph is one of the most disarmingly charming species that has ever roamed this earth. Every single person who's met him has at one point in their life had a crush on him. He's a goofily cheeky person, and a constant source of fun. Joseph has one of those faces that's impossible to get out of your head – a strong, wise nose, a smile so bewitching you'd believe it could solve inequality, and the lithe body of a Greek Olympian. He was a friend of friends, and a notorious womaniser. His need to take up space, which most people read as pure confidence, I read immediately as masculinity in crisis. The first time we met was during a university ski trip, and it took only about five seconds for us to be flirting in private. I was on this ski trip with a wonderful girlfriend from university – let's call her Sarah – and Joseph, right in front of me, made a move on her. Whenever they kissed, he opened an eye to check whether I was looking, as if he were suppressing and addressing his desires in one action. This performance of heterosexuality in an overtly public manner is also something I recognised, having grown up in a family which prioritised public expectation over the knotty truths. With my self-worth crumbling like a sandcastle on a rainy beach, Joseph's reminders of all the structures that already governed me – as well as his irresistibility – had me hooked. I was in the palm of his hands.

During that ski trip, I shared a bed with Sarah, and Joseph was in a nearby room. On the final night, Joseph asked if I would sleep in his bed so that he could sleep in mine with Sarah. I was only too happy to be used as his pawn (as well as to lie naked in a bed still warm from his own naked flesh). In the very early morning, when the room was still dark, I awoke to find Joseph crouched on top of me, his hand caressing my face, his teeth and eyes lit by the dawn. We looked at each other in silence, aware that it was only in this darkness that our intimacy could survive.

We went on a series of secret dates and formed quite a genuine, emotional bond. Joseph and I were in a sense total opposites, but I saw a great deal of myself in him. He talked to me about how parental expectation and pressures had instilled in him an obsessive academic drive, and how all of his anxieties came from a fear of disappointing his family. His ability to charm a room was a manifestation of his need to please everyone, lest he should be rejected, and this too I shared with him. Joseph was due to begin a seriously coveted placement in the surgical department of a hospital, and I sensed too that this derived not from passion but from a need to feel validated externally, all to cloak his suppressed queer desires. This is where Joseph and I really differed – he still had the favour of his family, and of society. To the external world, he appeared like the perfect Prince Charming. He was white, successful, straight and rich, privileges that he felt too scared ever to relinquish.

We both pitied each other, and we both envied each other. I pitied him for living a life that he didn't authentically choose, and for so fervently quashing all his desires – but I also envied him for the connection he still had with his family, and for all the signifiers of success he owned. I think he pitied me for so visibly failing the normative markers of social success, but envied my attempt to live an authentic life and pursue my own desires and creative ambitions. In fact, when we were walking around a festival together once – I was wearing some sort of metallic legging structure – Joseph couldn't believe the number of looks and homophobic remarks I got. 'Jesus, Amrou … I've never walked around and had this experience before. It's horrible. Do people always look at you funny?' 'I'm a genderqueer Arab living in Britain. Yes, Joseph,' I said, my hand cupping his warm testicles.

On our dates, it felt like we were each flirting with the other side of ourselves that we had in some way sacrificed. With me, Joseph got to dip his waters into queer nonconformism without having to sacrifice any of his privilege; with Joseph, I got to feel like I'd won a piece of the institution through getting him to desire me. There was a safety in the fact that our relationship only existed within the confines of our private dynamic – the construction of it meant that it wasn't really real, but more a rehearsal space for both our internal anxieties. It felt a bit like a reality show which no one was watching, as if we were on *Big Brother*, and the only two with the remote. Unlike in my relationship with Felix, my body didn't sweat with fear on the promise of intimacy, for it was always off the table. Thus, when Joseph dumped me with a polite but quite frankly dull and self-pitying WhatsApp message, I felt nothing. Feelings of nothingness became closely attached to all my sexual and 'romantic' endeavours. There was another boy I took a particular liking to in Cambridge – let's call him David. We were in a play together when he was in his final year and I was in my first year. David wasn't an immediately attractive man, but he was intelligent and sensitive, and had something gentle and protective about him; he was like a young Gandalf. The first-year/third-year dynamic was the perfect power structure to ignite my desires, and once again I wanted to be desired by a man who, in this very small context, was my 'superior'. As two queer people, David and I had a lot in common and became quite good friends. There was growing sexual chemistry between us throughout the rehearsals, so much so that every cast member remarked that it was an inevitability that David and I would sleep together.

After the party on the night of the final performance, I ended up sitting next to him in his bed at 5 a.m., our first sexual act surely seconds away. As I looked into his eyes, readying to kiss him, he said: 'Amrou. I wish I could. But I'm not attracted to men who aren't white. I think you're an amazing person, honestly … but there's something about white-on-white flesh I just find so beautiful.' Only years after the fact did I realise that this was something a Neo-Nazi would say – and I've recently told him as much – but at the time, I emptily agreed with him, and yet again felt nothing.

THE QUEER QURAN, AND OTHER QUANTUM CONTRADICTIONS

Leaving university was the first time in my life that I had properly been outside an institution. In my early childhood I had the institution of my family, once unconditional protectors, later omnipresent purveyors of my every move. For a lot of my life I had an unconditional faith in Allah, who also started as a source of love, and had then become a patriarchal watchman. Each of my schools, and Cambridge after them, also provided an institution to which I could aspire. I believed that my sense of belonging would come from my acceptance into such established structures. But coming to London after Cambridge was like being taken out of a playpen and thrown into a swamp of crocodiles. Suddenly, there was no structure on which to pin my hopes, no established rules to trust or reject. For even when I transgressed the rules of the institution I had grown up in, I had come to depend on the institution as a benchmark against which I could measure my behaviour. *Now what?*

After graduating from Cambridge, I rented a room in Camberwell advertised on Facebook by a friend of a friend (who luckily now happens to be one of the most wonderful people I've ever had in my life). I was now no longer speaking to my parents, besides a courteous monthly call, which consisted of 'How are you?' and 'Fine', apart from the very rare occasions when I had minus-3,000 pounds in my bank account and would call them for financial help. I no longer spoke to Majid or Lily, and was out of touch with Dennis for a little period. And my entire love life became confined to gay chemsex parties.

Technically, chemsex just means having sex on drugs, but in the last decade it has become a phenomenon among the gay community. Due to rising prices in cities, many queer spaces and gay bars have closed; this, coupled with the surge of Grindr, and other online gay hook-up apps, has taken sexual activity out of public spaces and into private homes. Chemsex parties tend to be organised through Grindr, and usually involve a group of men who don't know each other partying naked or in underwear at someone's house, taking copious amounts of drugs, having lots of sex, and pretending that time isn't real. Sometimes they can be quite enjoyable, but bleakness is always hovering close by, and it doesn't take much to fall over the precipice. Even though I never really had a good time at one, I grew somewhat addicted to them.

Whenever I was out at a gay club, side by side with hundreds of other queer people with whom I could potentially have found intimacy, I often ended up travelling to the middle of nowhere to attend a chemsex party I discovered on Grindr. This would especially be the case if there were people I fancied or felt a sexual chemistry with standing near me. The threat of rejection and fear of intimacy would turn my stomach into a cesspit of dread, and before I knew it I was having sex with multiple men high on drugs in a random person's house.

Now, there are many people who are able to attend these parties healthily, seeing them merely as an extension of their sexual identity, and a place to experiment and be liberated. I wish I were one of them. For me, they became the only place I felt I deserved to have sex, and the more drug-fuelled and zombified they were, the more affinity I had with them.

For the better part of sixteen months, the only sexual intercourse I had was confined to these settings. At one of them, I met a man who looked remarkably like Majid. Let's call him Tamar. Tamar was an accountant in his forties, rugged, Palestinian, and similar in frame to many of the male patriarchs in my family. Tamar messaged me on Grindr and invited me to a chemsex party he was hosting at his flat in Leyton. When I arrived, I found a pretty pathetic affair, more like a haunted house gone wrong. As soon as I entered, I saw a man syringe himself with some liquid crystal meth – called 'slamming'. It wasn't long before Tamar and I had locked ourselves in the toilet to have sex – and to get away from the vampiric gathering outside. It was hot and dirty, and he treated me like his subject. He became a recurring feature of my chemsex adventures, and I was always available to him for sex. No matter what I was doing, if Tamar invited me to one of his parties, I would drop everything to be there. And it's not like he showered me with attention when I went – I was one of multiple naked high gays roaming the darkened apartment, and there would be times he'd barely speak to me, or even tell me to just 'shut up'.

Once, I made the mistake of trying to embrace him. I bumped into him in a nightclub, and we decided to get a cab to his where another chemsex party awaited. In the back seat of the Uber, I tried to snuggle into his broad chest, which had the protective look of a gay Aslan. As I lay my head on his chest, I felt his stomach flinch, and the soft furry pillow I was hoping would provide some comfort became a cold bed of nails. Not wanting to address this colossal error, I stayed there for the entire cab journey, in what felt like an invisible choke-hold. When we got back to Tamar's flat, I was treated like a dog that had pooed inside the house. I was told to wait in his bed, where he would momentarily come to visit, before then going outside to have sex with one of the other people he openly found more desirable than me. Eventually, I fell asleep.

While I was out, Tamar clearly consumed a lot of G – a liquid drug that can give rise to epic episodes of horniness (and that can be fatal with alcohol) – and he came into the room and penetrated me as I was half asleep. I came to when I heard what he was saying; as he was fucking me, he was muttering, almost like a demonic incantation, 'You're nothing but my stupid fucking assistant.' Once the not-so-consensual office role-play finished, I fell back to sleep. I woke up to a WhatsApp message from Tamar telling me that he'd gone out to find guys, and to leave the house as soon as I got up and post his keys to him. Like Majid, he turned out to be a bit of a monster. It was the last I ever saw of him.

As I limped home through the Camberwell fog, all I felt was an extraordinary numbness. I was hollow. I think I felt an odd kind of resolution, as if the night's debasement correlated exactly with my sexual identity. It was like the first night I did drag, when I equated my queer identity with the filth on the floor. Only this time, it didn't hurt. For it merely proved something I had come to know and take as fact. I went to bed with a bizarre sense of satisfaction that I had proved myself right, and was content with the fact that at least I knew myself somewhat. But it was only a week later that I suffered a nervous breakdown of colossal proportions.

There were other challenges for me at this time. Although I had a good degree, I was in financial peril during the initial years after graduating. I was barely making anything as a performer, and was once again being seen for roles as terrorists. The only two jobs I got were for a 'terrorist's son' speaking only Moroccan (which is a different language to Arabic), and as an 'Indian friend' in a supermarket Christmas commercial. There was one glimmer of hope when I was invited to audition for the role of an Arab drag queen in a major TV series. I strutted to the casting in full drag, ready to give the performance of my life, which is when I was informed that the character was not a drag queen – indeed, he was a cold-blooded terrorist who wears a burqa to disguise the bombs. And so, in full drag, I had to mime a detonation sequence. *Low point.* Denim were also completely unknown on the London scene, and I was taking out credit cards to throw events so that we could make a name for ourselves (yes, I *still* have an appalling credit rating). Throughout the period after graduation, the invisibility became overwhelming, and the lack of institutional structures gave me nothing tangible to hold onto. *Where do I go for Christmas? If I died, would anyone notice? Do I have a family? I'm definitely not Arab, but I'm definitely not white. I like boys, but only if they don't like me or if they can't like me. I feel happy in dresses, but terrible when I take them off. And many people hate it if I put them on.* The combination of this instability with the ongoing chemsex parties and unloving urban brutality eventually had a surprising effect on me: I started to believe that I didn't exist. This isn't a metaphor. I genuinely believed I was not real.

The first episode that gave me the thought took place on a double-decker bus in London. I had got on it at 3 p.m. in the afternoon for absolutely no reason. I sat on the top deck by the middle, and there were only a couple of other people on the bus with me. In front to the left of me was a young female student with headphones, sleeping against the window, her jaw half open. A few seats behind me was a large man, who I realised was snorting a bit of cocaine on a key – he saw that I saw, and gave me a, 'whatever gets you through the day' look. *No judgement here, hun.* As the bus followed the route that was infinitely more structured than anything else I could have hoped for at that point in my life, I felt a slight tingle around the rim of my face, and my head felt very light, as if it might float off at any point. My stomach felt fluttery; less like butterfly wings, and more like a million locusts flapping their way out. The visual field around me became distorted, and eventually, my entire surroundings looked flat, like a 2-D drawing on an extremely thin piece of paper that was going to rip at any moment. It felt so real that I became panicked that this tear was suddenly going to appear, and in an instant there would be no one and nothingness. As my panic intensified, I was eventually thrust back out of the matrix, and into the 4-D world out of which I had almost evaporated. When I looked around me, I realised that the comatose student and highly alert businessman were gone, and that I was in Penge, the final stop of the London bus I had aimlessly taken.

It happened again, a few days later, and soon these episodes became more frequent, and much shorter. They were usually stimulated by moments of waiting or stasis. They were particularly common when standing in queues to purchase something, and ended when the person behind started shouting for me to move along. They became so common that I started to lose any sense of connection with reality, and instead to consider these episodes as real, actual events. I was once with a friend in a Caffè Nero, and as we waited in the queue, again I felt that the surroundings were imminently about to rip open and dissolve. When I finally got out of it and was being asked if I wanted milk in my coffee, I had no answer to give the barista. I knew that I preferred to have no milk with my coffee, but was unable or unwilling to open my mouth to express this. I simply turned to my friend and asked them to close the deal.

The frequency of these 'visions' grew rapidly, and, with very few things keeping me rooted to anything or anyone in reality, I began to take to heart what they were trying to tell me. It was as if my feelings of displacement and not belonging were being actualised, and I felt an acute sense of comfort that whatever it was that was guiding me towards these rips knew that I didn't belong in this world either. It was as if every feeling of not belonging had culmi- nated in this very simple solution: *of course I don't belong in this world. It isn't real.*

I had grown accustomed to feelings of displacement being extremely painful, of desperately wanting to join a group of people and wear their identity; now, I felt that everybody else was a fool for trusting in the fickle semblance of reality. How could they not see that the world they inhabited was no more than a fictional drawing that disguised something altogether different underneath? I had no idea what this something was, but I felt as if I was being pulled towards it. This tear in the surface of life, whatever it might be, had to be a wormhole to the *real*, to a site of new dimensions where my belonging could not be called into question. I just had to get to it. I tried closing my eyes during these episodes, hoping that when I opened them I would no longer be me, but a different kind of being in a different kind of place, perhaps even a starfish or an octopus, or something fluid and teeming with multiplicity.

These tears in reality, if I could only find them, seemed to open up the possibility of parallel universes living right under our noses, and I felt a physical pull towards them, as if they were caressing my hair, whispering in my ear a secret I couldn't quite make out. *Maybe this is Allah? Maybe this is some version of Allah I'd never known about?* In a period of my life where I felt so rudderless, this quest to find the rips gave me direction. I began to assume that I must be a prophet, who had been gifted with some semblance of a key that would unlock the truth.

By this point I had started avoiding friends entirely, and they were growing worried. I stopped answering calls, and my whereabouts were largely unknown to them. But once I realised I must be a prophet, it was my duty to let them know so that they could help me locate the rip in the fabric of the world that would redeem us all. And so I accepted an invitation to a dinner party, for most of which I sat in silence, internally pitying these unsuspecting mortals, who I might perhaps be able to save. Eventually, eyes turned on me.

'How have you been, Amrou?' *Well, I might not even BE, you know.*

'I'm OK. It's been a bit of a weird time.'

'What's wrong? Are you sick?' *Loaded question.*

'No. I've just been having these visions.' My group of white friends stared at me, embarrassed and concerned in equal measure, unsure as to the next move. And so I explained my quest to find the portal, and my theory that this world was a fictitious construct that could dissolve at any minute, and that I was a kind of prophet on the cusp of finding the elsewhere. There was an extended pause. *Please portal, come now. This is getting awkward.*

'Amrou, how many drugs have you been taking?' one of them asked. This connection hadn't occurred to me. I thought about it.

'Every weekend.' Another extended pause. A dear friend of mine from Cambridge then embraced me, and whispered, 'Oh, I'm so worried about you, Amrou.'

I went home that night a little bit unsure as to whether my visions were anything meaningful or merely a neurological malfunction because of my chemsex escapades. The next day, my father called to check on me. I really hadn't thought about him in a while, but when he asked me how

I was doing, I decided to try out the prophecy theory to hear his thoughts. After a pause long enough for me to make a cup of coffee, he then said, with an emotional warble in his voice:

'Amoura. Every day me and Mama worry that someone will find you hanging dead from a tree. It keeps us up at night. But ... we don't know how to help you. We don't understand you. Maybe we never will. But please ... just don't die. I'm going to send you some money tomorrow. Get therapy – or do whatever it takes so that me and Mama don't find you hanging from a tree. OK?'

After getting off the phone, I saw a message from my mother: 'Please take care of yourself habibi. Please. I love you so much.'

There were two things that helped me out of my dissociative delusions. The first was my extensive time in psychotherapy; the second was quantum physics. During my quest to reveal the ruptures in the fabric of reality, I wondered whether I was experiencing some manifestation of the universe's black holes. I began reading about these curious things that have bewitched physicists for so long, and this in turn led me to theories about how our universe might be only one in a series of multiverses. From there I stumbled on the possibility of parallel universes. This led me to read widely around quantum physics, in the hope that this might give me proof that my episodes were part of something that was actually happening. And in many ways, I discerned that what I was experiencing was, in a sense, 'real'.

Some brief context: quantum physics is a beautiful and strange sect of theoretical physics that caused quite a stir in the world of science in the twentieth century. Whereas standard Newtonian physics ostensibly studies observable reality on a macrocosmic scale, attempting to find the fixed scientific laws that govern our universe, quantum physics looks at the very smallest things in our universe. For quantum physicists, even atoms are huge; even the things that make up atoms – neutrons, protons and electrons – are huge. Quantum mechanics is interested in the subatomic particles inside neutrons, protons and electrons, particles like quarks, leptons, bosons and the Higgs bosons. The way that these subatomic particles behave has completely defied the standard fixed rules and formulae that we think govern the universe. Whereas classical physics treats particles like discrete, definite objects, quantum physics shows us that the idea of a particle being a fixed 'thing' is a construct.

One of the most famous experiments to demonstrate this is the double-slit experiment. The exercise is relatively simple; an electron is fired through a wall with two slits, and on the other side of the wall, the electron will leave a mark on either the left or right side of the reader. But every once in a while, the very same electron finds itself on both sides, having travelled through both holes on its journey. The *same* individual particle can be in two places at once.

How does this happen? Well, on a quantum level, we observe that a particle isn't really a particle at all – it's more like a wave carrying subatomic particles that behave quite chaotically. This discovery undermined the very structure of theoretical physics, and its quest to find order and the fixed formulae to understand resolute laws of our world. It let us understand that the very subatomic foundation of our world is anything but stable; it is always changing. Reality, as a result, is more an approximation of events – our brains can only observe a macro version of the very chaotic happenings really occurring at the core of things. What we are experiencing in 'reality' is just one of the events occurring at subatomic level; what is happening physically at the core of the thing we're observing often contradicts the actual thing we're observing. Quantum physics is scientific proof that reality really is constructed.

In the quantum foundation of our worlds, particles are nomadic creatures, roaming from party to party, and sometimes going to all at the same time (they're like particles with a really great chauffeur). Like shape-shifting scoundrels, they can often change their behaviour on being observed by a human, to alter their dynamics suddenly when we're no longer observing them. This isn't sci-fi fantasy, but the very foundation of our universe. It even hints that there is an infinite range of parallel universes around us all the time; if a particle can do multiple things at once, then perhaps we only inhabit one reality in a series of multiple universes.

The more I discovered about quantum physics, the less I felt that I was a prophet from another world. This quantum model of the universe was one that entirely made sense to me, and it allowed me to believe that I must belong to the universe. Once I realised that the laws of reality were merely a construct, at odds with the behaviours of the subatomic particles that actually comprise reality, then it struck me that surely all constructed notions of gender, racial hierarchy and identity were also imprisoning impositions. I was made up of trillions upon trillions of subatomic particles that basked in their multiplicity, existing as many things and in many places at once, and all the anxieties that had come to govern me came from restricting their natural behaviours. The very foundation of me could be a series of entanglements with no fixed direction; instead of hopping from social group to social group, could I exist in a subatomic state where I could find peace in the chaos of my conflicting identities?

At first, quantum physics can feel chaotic and overwhelming. Things behaving in a multitude of manners feels discombobulating, and navigating your way through it all is arduous and time-consuming. The road to my 'recovery' felt similarly so. Quantum physics teaches us that there are multiple versions of the same events happening all the time, and this is always the case all around us. We're just not aware of these, and become focused on a fixed, set version of reality to get us through our days. I, too, was chasing people and experiences that limited who I was, ignoring the multiplicity of options around me.

There was one person who hovered at my periphery at this time, and at first I didn't realise she could be such a saviour to me. She was a Saudi Arabian woman who had moved to the UK following her father's death, and was studying for a Fashion MA with one of the queens from Denim. Let's call her Layla. The first few times I met Layla, I had an aversion to her, of the same type that caused my hands to conceal my face whenever I came close to ejaculation. Her gestures reminded me of my relatives, and each time we interacted I broke into a cold, anxious sweat. The first time we met was at a friend's magazine party, and she came with Crystal, my wonderful sister from Denim. She was dressed like a true Arabian queen, the sparkly glints of her jewellery and Chanel handbag almost winking at me as she was ushered over. Layla's feline movements, melodic vocal intonations, and unreserved tactility reminded me of the women from the Middle East who I had all but obliterated from my consciousness. Back in the Middle East, kissing every person in the room with at *least* two kisses on the cheek was the norm (it was usually three, sometimes four). In the UK I had experienced socially dehydrated Brits flinch at my attempts at any more than one (and sometimes even just a hug), so had stopped doing it – but Layla, like a radiant ghost from my past, immediately settling into our shared cultural idiom, gave me three. As she did this, I felt my stomach constrict, as if my body was readying itself for a sudden escape; but I also felt something soften in my chest, as if silk was slowly expanding and caressing my insides. Eventually, I asked her: 'How's your course at Condé Nast going?' to which she replied, with the utter sincerity you'd usually find only in a Nutritional Wellness centre, 'It's a journey.' I immediately smiled, recognising yet another similarity she had with my mother – the ability to say *anything* with filmic melodrama. Throughout the night, I was both pulled towards and repelled by Layla, but always hovered around her perimeter, like a spaceship peeping at the tipping point of a black hole without wanting to get sucked in. I already knew on some level, this first night that I met her, that Layla would become someone I'd have in my life for ever.

Not only was Layla uproariously fun to be around, she had an unfiltered emotional purity that I found to be otherwise markedly absent in London. She wasn't scared to cry in public; she wasn't scared to shower you with kisses; she wasn't scared to share. But it took me a very long time to want to share anything at all with her. The first time I tried to distance myself from her was at a friend's concert. A pair of friends had set up a queer punk band, A Cinematic Masterpiece (ACM), whose gigs could make even Nigel Farage waltz in the street and campaign for a queer utopia. Their songs often told beautiful queer stories, such as of a transgender rocket ship who fled to outer space so that they could find a new home, falling in love with a comet on their encounter. The genius of their music is their use of catchy pop refrains so that an entire room can be united in the queer musical collectivity.

One rainy afternoon, Layla came to one of their concerts, in a 'garden' (it was more like a skip with brown foliage). When we were having a drink, she started talking to me in Arabic. She used the word 'habibi', and it felt as if she were lip-synching to a recording of my mother during my child-hood; as soon as she uttered the expression, her tongue became a snake wrapping itself around my throat. I smiled and said nothing. Layla was clearly excited at the prospect of being able to speak with another Arab at an event – especially one who was queer – and so continued. I under-stood everything she said, but the tightening grip of the python grew unbearable, and before I knew it, I snapped, shouting, 'Please stop talking to me in Arabic because I'm from the Middle East! I don't speak Arabic. I'm English, OK?!' Layla looked crestfallen. I hated myself for biting her head off like that, but also couldn't escape how strongly I felt. And so, for a while, I avoided her.

My interactions with Layla felt like a recycling of previous interactions that had only damaged me. I ignored the possibility that our relationship might be different, full of alternative outcomes, just like in quantum physics. So instead I reverted to a familiar pattern: I placed my trust in an institution, hoping that it might save me from my past.

It was at this point that I *properly* started my search for a boyfriend. I finally made the necessary shift from dating 'heterosexual' men to actual, living, gay people. A necessary switch. But it shames me to say that this phase of my London dating career comprised of only courting *white* gay men. It was my repeated compulsion to win the affection of gay men who reminded me of Mason, of people I automatically felt would never truly want me. *If I can convince these white Mr Darcys – no, not white poodles – to desire me as their boyfriend, then I'll really be worth something.* It is not uncommon for people of colour to spend their early dating careers fetishising white people (it is something I talk a lot about with my friends of colour). The reasons why this happens are complicated. For a start, the inherited shame that comes with being a person of colour in a racist society can warp your desires into looking for the thing that might compensate for this shame – in essence, a white badge of approval.

This can manifest in many different ways; an interesting historical example is from the Eighties/Nineties queer ballroom culture in New York. This thriving subculture comprised of Black and Latinx trans and queer people coming together to compete in pageants and Vogueing competitions (a queer dance form that blends breakdance with fashion-posing). Jennie Livingston's legendary documentary, *Paris is Burning*, shines a particularly fascinating light on the practice of 'realness', where members of the ball would dress up in 'Executive Realness,' attempting to imitate the corporate costumes of successful white middle class Americans. One of the interviewed drag queens explains, 'in real life, you can't get a job as an executive unless you have the educational background and the opportunity. Now, the fact that you are not an executive is merely because of the social standing of life. That is just the pure thing, black people have a hard time getting anywhere, and those that do are usually straight. In a ballroom, you can be anything you want. You're not really an executive, but you're looking like an executive, and therefore you are showing the straight world that I *can* be an executive. If I had the opportunity, I would be one. And that is like a fulfilment.' Whilst there is an inherent element of parody in the ballroom culture of 'realness', it's undeniable that many of those at the ball gain a validation from successfully emanating the ideal images of white America.

Till this day, the cisgender white male body has endured as the trophy within the gay community. And if you're someone, like me, who has a core belief that you are not worthy of love, you want desperately – as with the queens in the New York ballrooms – to wrap your hands around that trophy. It was in this mindset that I dated a series of white gay men who I felt it my mission to persuade to want me. And I was burned at every turn.

There was one boy, let's call him Alfie, who particularly stands out in my mind.

I had just finished a Denim performance in London, and was high off the adrenaline, my hands waving in the air like seaweed as I floated around a dance floor. I was in an orange, richly textured vest, in a face coated with highlighter and eyeliner, when I spotted Alfie looking at me from across the room. Alfie was *the* archetype of a fairy-tale Prince Charming – white, masculine, shaggy black hair with endearing facial features and a devilish little grin. I was drenched in the power of femininity that night, and it was as though this bewitched his contrasting masculinity; for before I knew it, he was moving slowly towards me, as if I was reeling in a fish.

The sex we had was enjoyable, and I could tell he was attracted to my femininity, as well as my race (he said he thought it was 'hot' that I was Arab; I'm not quite sure what he was expecting – for me to shout Allahu-Akbar on ejaculation?). There is a breed of white cisgender gay men who actively seek out effeminate boys (especially ones of colour) – I think it makes them feel more like a man to be dating someone occupying the traditionally 'feminine' position, and potentially even the racially less privileged one. Things, however, took a sharp turn when Alfie's masculinity and white entitlement came into crisis. The more we hung out, the more he realised that I was confident in my opinions, driven in my career, and unwilling to make myself small to accommodate him. I was dumped for being an 'intimidating' and 'aggressive' person. The blame fell to me for being 'intimidating', rather than to his white masculinity for being insecure – if I had taken up less space than him, I imagine our relationship might have had a better chance.

This was a pattern that repeated itself with a few white cisgender masculine men. They met me in a space when I presented as highly feminine, and they made a set of assumptions about me. But following our dates, when they ascertained that this femininity did not mean I was at all subservient or socially submissive, I was dumped for threatening their sense of masculinity. Perhaps there were also assumptions that I'd take up less space than my white counterparts because of my race. As a queer person of colour, people often assume you'll be smaller than they are. It's systemic conditioning – there are just so few representations of us that tell the world we're worth something. So when a queer person of colour seems to have more agency than the white people around them, we get labelled as 'aggressive'. But it's not we who are aggressive – what's aggressive is the system that conditions people to think that we don't deserve any space. In this period of dating, I learnt again and again that there were structures in place that wanted me to feel small.

This helped me realise that I was searching in the wrong places, and that the places where I belonged were not the places that I thought I wanted to belong. It was truly time to follow the quantum philosophy – instead of being fixed to identities in which I didn't fit, it was time to look a little differently. Perhaps the answers were around me in different ways, and I just hadn't noticed?

*

Soon afterwards, at a Denim performance in a club in East London, I completely flipped out, and it was all because of Layla. It was an exciting night for me. I had just signed with my wonderful agent, Kitty Laing – this was a real dream come true – and it was a sell-out show. During the performance, I came onto the stage, performing a comedy set and song about the rejection of my parents in the guise of a jazz song that turns into a scat-exorcism. Layla arrived and took her seat, now with short peroxide blonde hair and an all-metallic sartorial get-up that would have made my own mother proud. As the arts industry is dominated by white people, Layla and I were almost certainly the only two Arabs in a room of over 300 people. During my performance, Layla, who I subsequently learnt was drunk and also medicated on anxiety pills, began 'heckling' me in Arabic.

During my five-minute set piece, the heckling grew in volume and frequency, and it became difficult to get a line out without it being interrupted by one in Arabic. It felt to the rest of the room that I was being booed or insulted, but I was also the only one in that auditorium who understood what Layla was saying – most of her lines were ones of hyperbolic praise, of a kind of melodrama you would only find in Middle Eastern countries – 'my goddess, my dear love' and other such sayings. As this was occurring, I felt a serious fracture between the part of my identity that was performing to an almost entirely white audience, and the minuscule, completely weathered fragment inside of me that was listening to what Layla was saying. It felt as if the room were playing tug of war, with me as its rope, and the more Layla chanted, the more I felt a split. It became overwhelmingly painful, and really quite disorientating, and eventually, I screamed at the audience, and Layla in particular. I believe my exact words were 'SHUT THE FUCK UP'. As a performer, I had long known that getting angry at an audience was never a good idea; the fact that they are there implicitly means that they want you to succeed, and if your fuse blows and erupts in their direction, it upsets the safe performance contracts that give the audience faith that you are in control. When I screamed at Layla, it wasn't even a conscious decision; it happened by reflex, and I am told by friends who came to watch me that evening that it was really quite unsettling and confrontational. In all honesty, it put the whole room off.

After the show, I was extremely low. Not just because the night's performance had been impaired by Layla's interjections, but more because of my own behaviour. As the only Arab onstage, how could I have lowered myself to attack the only other Arab in the audience? Was my loyalty only with the white middle-class punters who fetishised my otherness for some Friday-night fun? I began to realise that my bodily convulsions every time someone spoke Arabic to me in a queer context were also indicative of a deeper problem I needed to confront. To find any kind of peace in having an identity so shattered, it was imperative I fuse together my queer identity and drag practice with my heritage.

A few days after the gig, I spoke to Layla. She had no recollection of what had happened at the gig, but was aware that she had caused a scene. Full of deep emotion and guilt, she apologised. I recognised the pain in her voice exactly; a kind of unresolved, childish fear. 'The thing is, Amrou,' Layla said, 'it's overwhelming for me to see you, another Arab, onstage being so confident, after everything I have been through … I think that's why I had that reaction.' Layla's family were conservative too, and much stricter than mine. She grew up in Saudi Arabia, where women are denied most of their agency, and where traditional codes of dress are a legality. After tragically losing her father to cancer, Layla inherited part of his fortune and moved to New York, before finally settling in London. Her relationship with her heritage is, like mine, complicated and confusing. Layla transgresses many of the gendered expectations of people in Saudi Arabia; to some serious pushback from her relatives, she set up an extraordinary fashion magazine called *Cause & Effect* that focusses on queer and trans bodies of colour, and she, like me, has suffered constant punishment at the hands of her family for pursuing an individual path that rejects the tried and tested ones everybody else has agreed to. So when she saw another 'runaway Arab' – this is what we call ourselves – performing defiantly in drag, she had the sudden impulse to use Arabic in a queer space, also searching for a way to bring this broken part of herself into this new, present, autonomous space. It felt as if we were two asteroids adrift, suddenly roaming in each other's orbits, each with the ability to help the other.

When we're suffering the aftershock of childhood traumas, there is invaluable remedy in connecting with other people. I believe very much in the promise of the chance encounter, that someone profound is always just around the corner, waiting to step into our lives at a time when we need them most. Maybe every human being is a prophet in some way for someone else, guarding some sort of answer, from the gargantuan to the microscopic, holding a key to our coming closer to resolution. Layla was in many ways an unexpected prophet to me.

Layla's experience in fashion meant that she was the perfect person to design the costumes for Denim's first music video. It was in this video that I first started looking to my Arab heritage to find inspiration for my drag. I was hesitant, at first. Drag had long been a vehicle for me to escape all the restrictive structures from my past – it was like a mute button, silencing all the things that I had been led to believe about myself. But I had explained to Layla how empty and fragile I felt without my drag armour, and I was always jealous of the empowerment my other queens had managed to find through drag in their everyday lives. Perhaps, I was starting to think, drag should also amplify our most deeply held fears and beliefs, rather than mute them, so that we can get them out in the open, and completely change our relationship with them. In conjunction with my weekly sessions in psychotherapy, it was time to use drag as a forum to deal with my past, and not just try to forget it.

Layla's costume design for me included a sapphire-blue belly-dancing duo, a blue velour tracksuit worn at some point by pretty much every young Arab woman who shops at Harrods, and a whole host of Middle Eastern accoutrements that made me feel as if I had skipped through one of the souks from my childhood and collected every single thing on my way. When I assessed the outfit in the mirror, I recognised myself in drag more than I ever had before – it didn't feel like I was wearing a mask, but rather a part of myself that I had long lost. I began to get emotional. I couldn't believe how much I looked like Mama. What a surprise it was to find in drag the image of exactly the woman I thought I was using drag to escape from.

When it came to finishing my make-up, I thought a lot about my mother's face. I wanted to emulate her regal beauty, and her unparalleled levels of glamour, and to capture the idea I had of her from before everything became difficult. For my entire life, my mother has drawn on a beauty spot with a brown pencil, and as a child, I became fixated as to its positioning. Ninety-nine per cent of the time the spot hovered above the left side of her lip, like a little signature that authenticated her star power; every now and then, she positioned it more on her cheek, as if the exaggerated placement were a little act of defiance, telling the world that she was unapologetically here and on her own terms (it was a tiny, but empowered moment of her political defiance). I went for the second option, and after I placed it and closed my eyes, it felt as if Mama was embracing me. As I took a deep breath, I could almost smell her, as though I was wearing a piece of her. When I opened my eyes, there was Layla in front of me, telling me in Arabic that I looked beautiful.

The shoot was one of the most enjoyable and moving experiences I'd ever had. Being in a queer space but dressed in an ensemble so rooted in where I came from allowed me to feel much more present in the experience – I wasn't simply hiding one side of myself to allow the other to succeed, but performing multiple facets of my identity simultaneously, like the quantum electron that moves through two holes at once. I felt a kind of cohesion I hadn't ever experienced before. There was so much about that weekend on set that reminded me of the Middle East – in a positive way. It was a collective experience, with every member of the drag troupe and our team coming together to create a joint piece of work.

This sense of community is something I missed acutely when I was living in London. Much of Western ideology is rooted in the pursuit of individual success (at the expense of others), whereas, while the tribal quality of community in the Middle East has its issues, there is also a joyous sense of warmth, kinsmanship and constant buzz to it. When I was a young child, every meal was an event, with relatives and friends coming together to feast and gossip; in the UK, I ate lonely ready meals, shivering in front of what seemed like endless period dramas. The Egyptian-inspired costume I wore was almost like a magical totem, merging the present room around me with memories of my past, including memories that I had only ever remembered as traumatic. As I danced in my costume, the beads smacked together to create a percussive soundscape, turning this white studio in East London into a Middle Eastern magical wonderland. The fabrics that Layla had put me in were remarkably tactile, as if each textile was a lost but happy memory from my past, hugging me here in London. This weekend catalysed the start of a journey – not to a new destination, but back to the very place I had started.

In drag, I could be the mama I had once idolised as a young child. I no longer wanted to think of my mother as a villain who wanted me shot – it was too painful to carry this around everywhere. I wanted to see her as a queen, as the fairy godmother she was during my stint as a gecko in *Cinderella*.

Most drag queens will tell you that they have a 'drag mother'. This is the queen who teaches you drag make-up and the delicate art of tucking away your penis, and who offers you a shoulder to cry on as you navigate the emotional turbulence of being a peacock in a world of lions. I never had a drag mother, and immediately assumed the role of drag mama to other fledgling queens without any real idea as to what I was doing. My drag mother was undoubtedly my own mother (even though she had no idea what she was teaching me). My mother could probably out-drag RuPaul; for her, every social event is an arena of external display, a battleground of designer garments, with every Arab woman trying to surpass the other with the most ostentatious and extravagant outfit.

She had the rare skill of holding the room's energy in the delicacy of her gestures, able to produce a laugh at very specific moments in the anecdotes she delighted with – and the more I worked with Layla on constructing Middle Eastern costumes, the more I looked into my memories to borrow my mother's behaviours for when I was entertaining a crowd onstage. The more I emulated her, the more success I had onstage too. What started as a sartorial shift quickly unlocked a whole perspective that allowed me to view my mother in the same way I had seen her in early childhood.

Around this time, there were two specific incidents that made me see how much more of a drag queen Mama was than me. Both of them happened around family weddings. Arab weddings usually send me into a spiral of self-loathing; none of my relatives can hide their pity for me, as if I will never be one of them because I'll never be married to a woman, have a regular job, or raise kids in a way they would deem acceptable. Usually I hide in a loo cubicle for three hours and answer all my emails. When that's finished, I watch porn.

I hadn't seen my parents in about six months, and we were all required to attend Majid's son's wedding. Majid and I still weren't talking, but the need to keep up appearances meant we swept the feud under the ever-bulging carpet. The day got off to a terrible start. My parents asked to meet me in a department store so they could purchase me a shirt that would disguise all my nonconformism. I loathe wearing plain suits and shirts – they feel like heterosexual prisons, the ties like death-penalty nooses. I often feel such an aversion to them that I can develop a rash around my neck. But I had learnt to just grin and bear it. So I agreed to wear the straitjacket, and dress up as the heterosexual son they all needed me to be.

When I went home to shower before the wedding, I applied my tattoo brightening soap to the unicorn on my chest as I always did. Caressing the unicorn's rump is remarkably soothing, and I can't leave the house without performing this ritual. I got ready for the wedding and left the house, and it was only after meeting my parents that I realised the soap had reacted to the painfully dull blue shirt and caused a bit of a stain. Mama's reaction deserved an Oscar nomination.

'Amrou! What is that?! We cannot show our faces with that!' *It's barely visible, Mother. And anyway, they already think we're all damned because I practise anal and wear heels.* Mama collapsed on the couch, breathing deeply. She was wearing a flowing black dress held together by a delicate metal circle frame around her neck. 'This is the last thing I need today. Of all days, today you do this.'

Mother, Trump is president. A slightly patchy section on an otherwise spotless shirt won't impair anyone's life. 'Do you know what I have been through today?' *Fuck, maybe it's serious, and this dirtied shirt is the final thing that pushed her over the edge.* 'This Valentino dress I'm wearing … it broke this morning. The metal neck fell apart. I had no other designer dresses that everyone hasn't already seen.' *OK, this is serious.* 'I was at my wit's end' – my parents sometimes like to throw in a British saying to show they belong here too – 'and I wouldn't have been able to go tonight if I hadn't found a welder to fix the dress for me.'

I felt a surge of euphoria as she said this. 'Why are you smiling like that?' my mother asked, apparently offended that I didn't empathise with the gravity of what she was saying.

'Are you telling me that you had to locate a welder to fix you into a designer dress so you could show your face at this wedding?'

'Yes, Amrou. It was very stressful. And now you come wearing a shirt that will make you seem like an orphan?' *A welder. A WELDER. Even the most avant-garde and exciting drag queens I know have never done anything as unashamedly drag as incorporating WELDING into their costume.* The only thing I could respond with was, 'Oh Mama … I love you.' I gave her a hug, to which she was half resistant, no doubt fearing that I might render the welder's hard work null and void.

My mother's behaviour at Arab weddings would make the perfect audition video for *RuPaul's Drag Race*, and the next one we attended together only confirmed her as the clear genetic foundation for my drag career. It was a cousin's wedding, and this time it was happening in Mykonos in Greece. (Side note: am I the only one who thinks weddings abroad are an absurdly selfish expectation on the part of the bride and groom, not least because they cost an absolute fortune?). The wedding took place over three days, the first of which was a 'tropical' themed party. The three-event itinerary meant that my mother was strategising months in advance, the trip more an opportunity to present a hat-trick of award season red-carpet ensembles than to actually celebrate the happy couple. Mama decided she needed a tropical themed headpiece to give her first place at party 1, but was struggling to find designers who could create one in the way that she had envisioned for her outfit. This is when she called me.

'Amoura … I was wondering … do you know where I can get a hat with fruits and plants on it? For the wedding?' *Yes, obviously. I basically sleep in such attire.* Now, the only thing I had ever heard my mother say about my drag was that it was the root of all her unhappiness; other than that, she pretended it didn't exist, and we never spoke about Denim or what I was up to. I knew that she'd never come to a drag show, or publicly show any support for it. But her calling me to ask if I knew any milliners with a flourish for the Copacabana ... well, I interpreted this as some kind of silent acceptance.

'Why, yes Mother ... I do. I have a friend who specialises in such things. Do you want me to take you to her studio?'

'OK. Why not.'

With the espionage tactics of one of Charlie's angels, I called my friend, telling her that I would be bringing my mother to her studio, but that all conversations about drag were strictly prohibited, and that the fact that she had worked with Denim in the past could not be brought up. I dressed in what was probably the dullest ensemble she had ever seen me in, and took Mama to her studio, a magical Narnia of hats bedecked with neon signs, Barbie dolls, and many other fabulous additions. The milliner and I acted like faint acquaintances, and I pretended that I was seeing these hats for the first time ever (when in fact I had already humped the floor in many of them).

Watching my mother try on hats that I had only recently performed in was pretty disorientating. It felt like a scene from an Almodóvar film, where many different layers of performance were occurring simultaneously; my mother, walking around the studio, was someone who I effectively impersonated onstage, wearing the same hats that she was now trying on, and she right now was like a version of Glamrou but in real life, with all of this left unsaid in an entangled merging of realities. *Very quantum.* Mama eventually selected a leopard-print hat that had a huge tropical leaf towering above it like a skyscraper, and which had to be placed in a box as big as an adult human.

To save money, we booked our flights on easyJet (even though the absurd hat cost more than our return flights). Mama hadn't got the memo that easyJet didn't offer first-class service, and she arrived at the airport with a different suitcase for each separate outfit. The foliage-centred hat had its own altogether. So when it was time to check in, Mama was utterly baffled that she was being charged through the roof for all the extra baggage. With no respect for the British passengers all grumbling in the queue behind her, Mama threw a gloriously melodramatic strop that made me want to get my popcorn out. The engrossing heroine monologue ended with Mama shouting, at full volume and with her arm raised in the air like a barrister going in for the kill: 'This is not easyJet. THIS IS DIFFICULT JET!' At this, she got a round of applause from everyone waiting behind her, and the faintest hint of a smile creased her lips. What a queen.

As I started to understand how much of my drag vernacular was passed down to me from my mother, I decided to investigate this artistically (and no, not through another canvas where my mother crumbles in front of the collapsing Twin Towers). Inspired by the nickname Layla and I had given each other, I made a short film called *Run(a)way Arab*, which is about a young Arab boy watching his mother get ready to go out, spliced with this same character twenty years later, preparing for a drag performance while reminiscing over their mother. The entire experience was trippy beyond belief. My parents own a property in London, which they use whenever they visit (especially Mama, for work). I was not allowed a key to the property, for fear that I might upset the perfectly arranged interior with my queer anarchism. I was paying for the short film myself, and so the budget was basically non-existent, and it was a struggle finding an authentic Arab interior, not to mention a wardrobe befitting the character based on my mother. I begged my parents to give me a key so that I could occasionally use the house as an 'office space', and after some hard negotiation, I was given one. As soon as my parents were out of town, we raided the interior.

The shoot weekend was one of the most stressful creative experiences of my life. Almost immediately after my parents drove to the airport, a truck of camera equipment and a twenty-person crew rocked up and marched their way into this aesthetically refined opulent interior. We took pictures of absolutely everything – even the way the jewellery was laid out on the table – because my mother's obsessive eye would be able to discern if even a stitch was out of place. Then a hefty crew of film people, with all kinds of obtrusive equipment and scaffolding, marched into the house, moving everything about, while I pretended to be as calm as a cucumber (when actually I had to go and meditate in the bathroom every hour to stave off panic attacks).

We had already filmed the drag sequence, and the day in the house focussed on the young Arab boy watching his mother get ready. The mother character asks her son for advice on her outfit, (as my mother used to ask me in our private ceremonies in the Middle East), before leaving to greet some guests. When she goes out, the young boy imitates the make-up of his mother as a way to feel close to her, but when his mother discovers this, she is mortified in front of her guests and this makes her furious. The actress playing my mother looked like my mother, and wore my real mother's clothes in my real mother's bedroom; the young boy playing the young version of me actually looked like my child self. I watched most of the scenes in my mother's closet on the director's monitor, as if I were viewing footage from my past, and every layer of what was real or what was constructed collapsed in on me. Layla, who had designed the costumes for the film, was by my side holding my hand, and I wouldn't have been able to get through the day without her.

Watching the child gaze on his mother in fascination, putting on make-up out of love and curiosity, only then to be scolded, was completely illuminating for me. As I watched the little boy respond on the monitor, it became utterly clear – he was only a child. *I was only a child when I was being made to feel that I was a problem.* Watching this encounter from an objective distance, it was so obvious. In the lucky (and probably unlikely) event you have access to a willing cast of actors and a set like a scene from your childhood frozen in time, I would genuinely encourage any of you trying to work out your feelings around a difficult childhood to re-stage it with actors and watch it on playback. Otherwise, trying to see your memories is like trying to get a full view of a hand that's planted on your face. Your perspective is all over the place.

For all my life, I have carried around a deep sense of blame – *my parents are sad because of me*. One of my biggest fears is that I've upset people. If someone is slow getting back to me on a text, I rack my brain, wondering what I could have possibly done to upset them and lose their friendship. *Is it that time I was a bit tired and seemed cold after that play? Is it because I didn't give them enough eye contact at their dinner party? Do they somehow know that I lied about liking that film? Have they figured out that I'm a total imposter?*

Even after years of being represented by wonderful, endlessly supportive agents, every time I get a phone call or an email from them, my immediate assumption is that I've done something that's warranted me getting dropped. Every. Single. Time. The belief that my problematic behaviours caused my parents to reject me means that every possible scenario I enter is an opportunity where something that I do might cause me to be rejected. Even when I go on stage, the prospective audience is never a potential source of support, but an inevitable well of disappointment in me. But, as I watched the monitor in my mother's closet, I began to see something different.

The boy who was cast as my mini-me had never acted before. He had one of those expressions that was so innocent it made you want to bundle him up and protect him from all of the infinite horrors of the world. His eyes were large and curious, taking in everything around him with a totally open sensitivity. Directing kids can be challenging, but when the stars align, I find it can be a lot easier than directing an adult. They can be far less self-conscious and concerned with their decisions as an actor, and just perform the task of the scene, totally unfiltered, and completely in the present scenario.

He was one of those actors, and in every single take, he responded to the woman playing his mother with complete sincerity, as if it were really happening. Observing the monitor, it seemed that the boy watching his mother put on make-up was observing only out of love and awe; and when he went to try on the make-up, it was with an utterly innocent curiosity. I had imagined this scene to have more dramatic gravitas, but as the boy played the scene with complete naturalism, his applying make-up felt completely playful, and not at all transgressive.

I had internalised the feeling that my penchant for make-up was an aberration, but watching it from one step removed, it felt like anything but. Wearing make-up was an act that caused extreme conflict within my family – but here on the screen the act was utterly pure. When we got to the scene in which the young boy is berated by his mother for trying on her make-up and clothes, I saw, from my seat in Mama's closet, how confusing this was for the young boy. When I asked him what he was feeling in the scene, he said: 'Confused. Just earlier she wanted me to give advice on her clothes. So why did she get angry all of a sudden?' I then asked him why he thought his character put on the make-up. After I asked this, he looked at the floor for such a long time that I started to think that he might have pooed in his pants and was trying to formulate an escape plan. But then he looked up at me and said, 'Because he loves his mother and wants to be like her.' I excused myself, locked myself in Mama's closet, and cried all over her furs and embroidered textiles. All I could think was: *None of this was my fault.*

After filming *Run(a)way Arab*, I began to feel something quite foreign to me: anger at other people. I had long been accustomed to flagellating myself, over forgotten commas, say, or for achieving anything less than 100 per cent in all academic and professional endeavours. Normally it was hard for me ever to be angry at other people. Such a position would suggest that I had enough self-love to be enraged that someone else had potentially injured it, whereas I approached every scenario as someone unworthy of love, and just felt appreciative of anything that resembled it, even when it quite clearly wasn't. Now, however, I suddenly started to feel mad at others.

This was unexpected, because I was creating work to try to find the joy in things. Drag, in particular, was about rediscovering the aspects of my heritage and my mother that I wanted to think about in new, positive, queer ways.

Drag was becoming a vehicle in which I could live out the feminine parts of my upbringing from which I had long been severed. I had no real intention of diving back into the parts of my life that traumatised me, but, like with *Run(a) way Arab*, I was being led to them. For, of course, the more difficult memories hovered side by side with the ones I was exploring – like quantum contradictions – and it wasn't long before they clashed together and engulfed me. The resulting energy was a fiery fury.

I was no longer willing to believe that I was the cause of the world's anger. I wanted to be able to enter a social situation without the paranoia that my merely being there might cause even a pint of beer to reject me. And so, instead of harbouring the belief that I was the root of my parents' unhappiness, I forced myself to believe that they were the cause of mine. During therapy, I recounted every single thing that they had done that had actively contributed to my poor mental health and the shame surrounding my sexuality and identity. The list seemed endless ... *Their reaction to my intention to marry Macaulay Culkin? Their terrifying responses to my watching gay TV and cinema? When they threw away my favourite clothes? When they told me that I was unworthy of love? The way they emotionally manipulated me into thinking that my queerness was to blame for their problems? The way they allowed me to internalise some Islamic attitudes towards homosexuality?* But then again ... they did make huge sacrifices for me to have the life that I had. Mama, though sometimes cruel, was incredibly warm and funny, and so much of what I loved about drag was rooted in her. But, like the whack-a-mole arcade game, I had to hammer down any thoughts that popped up that made me think of them fondly – for the time being, I needed to picture them as villains who had constructed a world of unhappiness for me, otherwise the feelings of shame that came from believing I was to blame would never disappear. During this month, I rejected every single call from Mama and my father, I ignored every text, and I diverted every email of theirs into the trash. One day, Mama called me twenty-one times, clearly worried for my safety. Eventually, I picked up.

'Amoura. Habibi. I am so worried about you. Why have you been ignoring me and Baba?'

'Because I don't want to speak to you.' *Gosh, that felt satisfying.*

'What do you mean by that?'

'I mean I don't want to speak to you. Whenever I speak to you, I feel shit.'

'…' *Weren't expecting that, were you?!*

'For my entire life you have made me feel so bad for being gay and for being myself. You told me I was the source of your unhappiness. Well you know what, you are the source of mine. For so long you have made me feel ashamed for being myself. I don't need you and Dad any more. So why should I put up with your beliefs? Unless you and Dad are willing to apologise for what you have put me through, I have nothing to say to you.'

Long pause.

'Amrou. You are so lucky to have generous parents like me and your father. Any parent would have reacted the way we did to everything you were doing.'

'Actually, no Mum. What you did was fucking homophobic and has made me a paranoid, often depressed person with severe mental health issues. Most parents would be proud of a kid who has had the life that I have – you're only embarrassed.'

'You know where we're from. What do you expect?'

'Are you willing to accept blame for what has happened?'

'No, Amrou. We're your parents. We don't have to apologise to you. We did the best we could.'

'OK then. Please never call me again.'

'As you wish.'

As I was about to hang up the phone, my mother interjected with one final remark – the only bit that sounded from the heart (everything else felt culturally scripted): 'Amrou. I just want you to know that I love you. And whenever you need me, I am here.'

'I don't need you any more.'

I hung up the phone.

It was six months before I spoke to her or my father again. I told them not to contact me unless they were ready to apologise, or just to wait until if or when I was ready to make contact. This decision gave me emotional space. The combined love and resentment I had for my parents was so muddled, and everything I did felt in some way a form of disappointment to them. Any time I got some promising career news, I only felt anxious that they would discover it was about something queer. Any time a photo of me in drag circulated on the Internet, I felt scared it would fall into their hands. I had reached pure financial independence from them a little while ago, and needed to sever myself from them to feel completely autonomous, to have a chance to feel proud of myself for my work, rather than harbouring a constant buzz of shame around it. Throughout that six months though, I realised how desperate I was for them just to say, 'I'm sorry'. It was in this period that my brother and I became close in a way we had never been before.

I really love my brother, but I don't know him as well as you might expect for twins. We spent our time in the Middle East separated by our mother and father; we went to different schools from the age of twelve, and lived in different countries during our twenties. But my kind, generous, wonderful brother had recently moved back to London, and my mother was visiting him during my decision to make a clean break from her. Throughout the six months, Ramy was a pillar of support for me, at every stage assuring me that my feelings were true and valid, and keeping me up to date on how my parents were responding. I became hooked on the sequence of events, as though my life were a Netflix drama. Here is the chain of events that went down with Mama and Ramy:

Episode 1 – *Anger*: Ramy said that as soon as I got off the phone with Mama, she raged around the living room, furious that I would dare to attack her for being a bad parent. I wish I could have watched this impassioned performance, which included such hyperbolic claims as, 'I am the best mother in the world'; 'how dare Amrou accuse me of this when it is Amrou who made me unhappy all my life'; and, with utter seriousness and self-belief: 'I am perfect'.

This was the reaction I assumed she'd have. Whenever any critique came her way, her go-to response was that she was a person without flaws. As much as I admired the goddess complex, it automatically made everyone else at fault. She so vehemently believed that she was the ideal mother and person, that by proxy you were always in the wrong. Mama was good at gaslighting, but also an expert emotional manipulator; it didn't take long for her eyes to water, and for her to spin out gut-wrenchingly guilt-tripping phrases like 'I sacrificed my life for you', and 'I only ever wanted you to be happy'. So I was unsurprised that this was her initial response with Ramy, but still hurt that she couldn't see that anything that she had said to me in my past was unacceptable. She told me I wasn't worthy of love – surely that had to get me an apology Post-it note at the very least?

Episode 2 – *Devastation*: The next time Ramy spoke to Mama about the entire scenario, he acted like my lawyer, vouching that the way she and Dad attempted to control and eradicate my sexuality and queer identity was emotionally abusive, and tried to explain the consequences this had had in my life. What started as my mother shouting at my brother and refusing to believe what he was saying turned into her collapsing on his bed and weeping. Ramy said that she was completely broken when she realised that she might have had any role in making me unhappy. According to Ramy, her reaction was difficult to articulate – she was heartbroken that anything she had done had caused me so much pain, but still firmly believed that what she did was right regardless.

Hearing of my beautiful, dainty mother falling down with grief was a horrible picture to come to terms with. I immediately felt guilty, and wanted nothing more than to run to her house and beg her not to be upset. I was also moved that any notion of my unhappiness could elicit such a primal response in her – *maybe she really does want me to be happy?* But these feelings were muddied by a latent rage on my part, for the fact that she still couldn't apologise for the things that had hurt me so much. 'Sure, she's upset,' I told Ramy. 'But is she sorry?'

'I don't know bro. But she's really depressed … she can't get out of bed. She's crying a lot. I don't think she realised how bad it was. I think she's pretty shell-shocked to be honest. I've never seen her like this.' Again, the idea of my mother being so depressed was painful … but it was also oddly satisfying. It sounds emotionally stunted, but I got an odd kind of pleasure from the idea that I was punishing her somewhat. Finally, *she* was feeling some hurt, and perhaps this might be a way for me to shed how much I had punished myself. *Let her be sad. She deserves to be in pain over what's happened. It can't all be my fault.*

Episode 3 – *Victim*: According to Ramy, my father had no interest in playing along. At this point in his life, he was suffering a deep depression. He had lost a great deal of his fortune in the recession, his business had completely collapsed, and he had been forced to move to Dubai to work tirelessly in a completely new job. Now I know I've painted my father in quite a negative light so far, but he really is a very good man. He's just extremely tired. He left Iraq in his late teens to study in the UK, then had to move back to Iraq, hopping around jobs in the Middle East, before working his socks off to build a small fortune in the UK from nothing, sacrificing everything so that my brother and I could have a good life – and I'm eternally grateful to him. He learnt English from scratch, and worked in telecommunications even though he had no passion for it; his dream of becoming a footballer almost came true when he was scouted to trial for Arsenal football club, only to sustain a leg injury that required complex surgery and left him with a life-long impairment. When he wasn't working, he wanted things to be easy. My nonconformism made things difficult for him.

Baba was essentially far too miserable and tired to engage in anything at all self-reflective, and he told my brother and my mother that he wouldn't hear a thing about me being angry at them. His argument was this: 'I work like a dog. I'm unhappy. And now I have this ungrateful little shit telling me that I was a bad father?' According to Ramy, Mama was trying to work through the issue, slowly coming to understand why what had ensued in our childhood was so emotionally damaging to me. But any time she raised it with my father, he screamed for her to shut up, telling her that my silliness was not to be entertained. 'Dad's really depressed bro. He's not gonna tolerate any of this,' Ramy told me.

During my conversations with Ramy at about this point, it dawned on me just how difficult a husband my dad must have been for my mother. Mama was actually trying to work out how to salvage the relationship between us, while my father wasn't at all willing. In fact, he was trying to forbid my mother from apologising for their attitudes towards my sexuality in my upbringing. What I had failed to see all my life was that my mother was also a victim of the Arab male patriarchy. *How much of what she said was silently puppeteered by my father?* I mean, she's a woman who was raised in male-controlled countries. How much of what she did to control me was a result of her having led a life that was controlled by men?

My mother was on the receiving end of so much of the anger I felt about my childhood. It didn't ever occur to me that she and I might be ensnared within the same system of oppression. In fact, in Middle Eastern households, you'll often find the mother as the mouthpiece of the patriarchy;

while the father silently benefits from his male privilege, the women are left to enact the structures that the men profit from, perhaps even dictate. My dad's apathetic response to this entire odyssey pointed to the fact that it mostly fell on my mother to be the bearer of the patriarchal hand – as such, I had always punished her more in my mind. But according to my brother, she was left once again to deal with the consequences of what was happening. My brother, who had always worshipped my father, said that this entire period had given him a whole new respect for Mama, and for what she had had to deal with.

After six months, I received this message from Mama: 'I'm so sorry you feel so bitter. If I hurt you or upset u in the past it was because of my ignorance and emotions and I'm genuinely very sorry. I always tried to do my best but I'm not perfect. Nobody is. I love you and can't live without you so pls let us start a new page. All I want is your and Ramy's happiness. I have nothing else.'

She had apologised. And in an authentic way that allowed me to believe that she really meant it. She wasn't apologising in a way that suggested her actions were intentionally harmful – as a woman raised in a Middle Eastern Muslim family, she had genuinely done the best that she could. She believed that homosexuality was a sin that would throw me *and her* into hell, and she wanted to protect me from the flames. She knew that the community would turn on me for being queer, and was desperate to prevent my exile. My mother is a very beautiful and innocent soul; she's never touched drugs, and the most transgressive thing she's done in her life is buy a ticket for Cirque du Soleil. The path I was taking quite clearly terrified her, and she was doing whatever she could to keep me on the only one she believed was safe. Sure, it wasn't the right tactic, but it was all she knew. And here she said it – she wanted us to start a new chapter. I appreciated that she knew we might not be able to erase the damage of our history. But maybe we could begin a new relationship, starting now. The next day, Mama and I went for lunch.

To mark this new chapter, I wore something I would have previously been too scared to wear in front of Mama, especially at a fancy restaurant: a rayon pyjama trouser and shirt duo bedecked with pictures of an unknown woman, bright blue high-heeled ankle boots, and a jacket patterned with fluorescent clouds. The sound of my heels against the marble floor echoed that of my mother's as a child. I was led towards the table, but Mama wasn't there. I got paranoid that she might have seen my outfit and done a runner, but after five minutes she was ushered over to the table, in a serious mood with the waiter. As she sat down, wearing sunglasses as big as her face – even though we were indoors and it was raining outside – she commented, with the gravity of a doctor breaking fatally bad news, 'They sent me to the wrong table for ten minutes. I've never been treated like this in my life.' A warmth flooded me, and I said, 'Oh Mama. I've missed you so much.'

'I've missed you too, Amoura.' We held each other's hands across the table.

'Do you like what I'm wearing?' I asked, both jokingly and provocatively. Mama considered her response, not wanting to damage this newly erected bridge between us.

'Not really,' she said lightly, still holding my hands. 'But you should wear what makes you happy.' This felt like a landmark moment between us. My silent punishment had been an attempt to establish new parameters between us – and the experiment had worked! Did I change her mind about what she thought was acceptable for a Muslim boy? No. But did she make the decision to bypass her beliefs so that we could be together? Yes. And that was the most accepting thing I had ever experienced from her.

The lunch was one of the most honest and open times I'd ever had with Mama. We talked about drag, and how in many ways my drag was tied to her. True to form, when I teased her about the hilarity of hiring a welder to fix her dress, she responded with utter sincerity: 'What's funny, Amrou? It was a very stressful day.' I asked her why she had tried so hard to prohibit my drag, and her answer blew me away.

'Amrou. Amrou. You are so lucky to be a man.' I was going to interject that I don't identify as a man, but she quickly continued. 'Do you know what I have had to suffer because I am a woman? Do you know how hard life is as a woman? Your Baba treats me like shit, he doesn't let me talk, and he screams at me whenever I try and communicate with him. The men in our family have stolen money from my business and just expect me to stay quiet because I am a woman. Being a woman is hell. And you, my special Amoura, with your special brain, choose to be a woman, even though you are lucky enough to be a man? I don't understand it.' Now there's a great deal to unpack here. It took a while to make her see that for some people born male, their male body isn't a 'gift', but a burden that makes them feel dysphoric and out of place in their own bodies. It took even longer to explain that drag isn't about 'being a woman', but about expressing a side of yourself that you feel has been trapped, and if anything it parodies gender construction, rather than enforcing or replicating it. But oddly, it didn't take long for her to understand how drag was my way to stay close to the Middle East, how it helped me remember the feminine aspects of our culture and my times with Mama long ago. But she was resolute that she would never fully understand my love of drag, and was honest that she'd never come to a show or outwardly support this – this wasn't said out of malice, only truthfulness and love. Again, I began to understand the lengths to which she had been a victim of the patriarchy, and how my ability to transgress was in her eyes a patriarchal privilege. 'If you had been a woman, you wouldn't get away with what you do,' she said. I told her that I wasn't willing to feel grateful for having suffered what was in her eyes 'only a small amount of trauma'.

'Amrou … you are so lucky.' When Mama said this, it was clear she didn't mean that I was lucky to have suffered less than I could have. It seemed to come from genuine jealousy. As Mama and I gazed at each other, it became perfectly clear that so much of her behaviour towards my autonomy in life was a projection of the fact that she'd never fully had her own. With the pressure to adhere to the collective rules of the Middle Eastern tribe, it is rare for any individual truly to establish their own path within it. The desire to prohibit this comes both out of preservation, but also resentment – 'if none of us get to live by our own rules, then who the hell are you to?' My queer independence, that for so long had been portrayed as the *cause* of the tribe's unhappiness, was actually just a reflection of it that made them notice it all the more. 'And I'll give you this,' Mama continued. 'You are very brave. Even if I don't agree with what you do, no one can say that you are not brave.' This was an extraordinarily reparative thing to hear. My mother, regardless of her cultural attitudes, and all her past attempts to prohibit my nonconformism, could still appreciate how hard it had been for me to live an authentic life. And it was her way of telling me she was proud of me. Over the course of the lunch, Mama and I forgave each other for everything that had been said in the past, and made a vow that we would treat each other more kindly in the next chapter of our love story.

As I walked her to a taxi – which was only taking her *DOWN THE ROAD* – I talked to Mama about how we were both victims of the patriarchy. 'I mean, how fucked up is it that sins on our left shoulder get ten points, while good deeds only get one? Isn't that ridiculous?' For as long as I remember, I had believed that each sin was worth ten points, while each good deed was worth one, meaning that there were about a trillion times as many points on my left shoulder than on my right (spookily, every chiropractor I've visited has commented that my left shoulder is much tighter than my right). With an almost mystical calm, as if she were a deity about to disappear right in front of me, Mama said, 'You've remembered that wrong, habibi. A good deed is worth ten points. A sin is only worth one.' She stepped into the taxi as though it were a private jet, and just before it drove away, she told me that she loved mc.

The negative cycles of thoughts that had come to govern my brain seemed also to have polluted my memories. Islam, particularly, had been reduced to something I only ever thought of as *bad*. Every neurological pathway that started with Islam always led to feelings of shame and worthlessness, and an image of eternal incineration. Anything that reminded me of Islam made me feel a sharp stab, so much so that I had no clarity whenever I actually thought about it – it was just a vague and enormous dark cloud of something ominous that I was too scared to look at closely. Out of the fog, however, Mama had rescued a specificity that had got lost in this pixelated dark image – that sins were only worth one point, and good deeds were worth ten. *How could I have remembered this wrong? For all my life I had remembered this the other way around.* Allah might not have been a punitive dictator taking relish in my misery. What if Allah was a force that wanted me to do good? What if Allah wanted us to find out that the good was always worth more? *Does Allah maybe think I'm good on the inside?*

I began reflecting on how this tied in with my whole life. While there was a great deal of pain growing up, especially around my sexuality and gender, there was always some good that came from this pain. Fears of failure somehow manifested in success. Rejection and exclusion led to finding drag, which is quite honestly the thing that saved my life. And drag brought me love of all different kinds – a love of other queer people, a self-love, and, in a surprising turn of events, a love of my heritage. By this point, I was dressing as my mother pretty much every time I was in drag, and through Layla I was becoming closer to my heritage than I had ever been. Perhaps I was ready to do the same with Islam?

It was at around this time that I met the Muslim women after my show in Edinburgh. It felt to me that Allah had placed these prophetic women to show me something, and all I could hear the morning after was the calming, restorative words of the beautiful girl in the hijab holding my hand. 'Glamrou. Allah loves you.'

I soon began to form close ties with the QTIPOC+ communities in London (Queer, Trans & Intersex People of Colour). Victoria Sin, the non-binary drag queen I mentioned previously, became a close friend of mine, and we even collaborated on a film together. As much as a dear friend, Victoria Sin is a hero to me. They are a non-binary drag performer with Asian heritage, and initiated a project to bring QTIPOC+ people together in London. I couldn't believe that I could occupy a space with so many other queer bodies who were also from minority ethnic groups, and this became a significant source of solace for me. Through these networks, I met a remarkable make-up artist, Umber Ghauri, who identifies as queer and Muslim, and learnt so much through them – in particular, about how they've been able to reconcile their queer and Muslim identities. As Umber taught me, the Quran is teeming with queer possibilities. Now I'm not saying that the Quran is a guidebook to a queer utopia, because, like many religious texts, it has its fair share of hegemonic rules and restrictions. But it is also an extraordinarily poetic work, with a diverse range of thoughts, many of which feel compatible with being queer.

Prophet Muhammed once said, 'Islam began as something strange and will return to being something strange, so give blessings to those who are strange.' *Amen Muhammed!* If you replace the world Islam with 'people', the sentence could feasibly be the slogan for a queer sex-positive disco in Berlin. As I had learnt from first-hand experience, the West has limited most people's perceptions of what a Muslim looks like – we're either terrorists, terrifying, or terrified. Cultural representation has a lot to answer for here; pretty much every Arab actor will tell you that since 9/11, they've been in business, but for the wrong reason. American networks, in particular, are hooked on narratives where white male soldiers gun down Arabs like we're vermin. So it's unsurprising that most people would find the idea of the Quran having pockets of queerness as ludicrous as Katy Perry's claims to cultural authenticity (the right-wing media has made a particular meal out of positioning Islam as a complete threat to Western civil rights) – but ideas about Islam are limited, and mask the subatomic complexities hidden deep inside the faith.

On my rereadings of the Quran, I came across this passage about Allah. It says that Allah is the 'One who shapes you in the womb as He Pleases.' (Quran 3:6), and that 'of His signs is the creation of the heavens and the earth and the differences of your tongues and colours' (Quran 30:22). When I came across this, it was the first time in my life that I felt connected to the Quran without an urge to repel it. I could just hold the book as though it was meant to be in my hands, like a calm, sleeping kitten. There it was, in this ancient 'evil' text, the idea that variance and difference among human bodies was all part of Allah's plan. Perhaps Allah views human beings in the same way I used to think about marine aquatics – as a collection of ever-changing, different bodies, all coexisting as a form-less mass unified by light and love. I had only ever pictured Allah as a fascistic punisher who built the world on strict rigid lines – but the more I discovered about Islam, the less this seemed to be the case.

I reached out to a queer Muslim group I had heard about, a community set up for those wanting to merge their faith with their queer identity, and who find Quranic justification for queer identities. I was invited to one of their events, and eventually plucked up the courage to go along. The meeting took place on a mellow autumnal Sunday, and as I got on the bus to the café where it was being held, I smiled at the idea that I was willingly heading towards an Islamic event, when for so long in my life I had been running away from them. I was actively seeking out Islam, no longer attempting to eradicate it from my system. The event was one of the most welcoming spaces I had ever been in – so free from judgement, so free from fear, instead offering an environment rooted in Islamic concepts of love and togetherness. We sat around three little tables that were brought together to make one clunky big one, and I looked around, taking in the diversity of identities around me. There were Muslim men in female Islamic robes and a trans woman wearing a hijab, and I thought about little Amrou in Islam class, and how I wished I could tell them that one day they'd be sitting in a room full of other queer Muslims, and that love, not eternal fire, awaited them.

The three-hour meeting was centred on the Islamic concept of Wilayah. Wilayah translates as 'spiritual advisor', and more conservative readings of the Quran interpret it as the practice whereby Muslim men ensure women are marrying appropriate Muslims. But the various Quranic passages, on further reading, reveal a different meaning to the one patriarchal Islam has reduced it to. Here's the one I found most comforting:

And the masculine people of faith and the feminine people of faith are spiritual protectors of one another: they encourage what is right and discourage what is wrong. (Quran 9:71)

We set off in different working groups to discuss how these readings might apply to us as queer people. The more I read, and the more I discussed, the more I realised that I practised Wilayah with my queer drag family, Denim. For me, part of identifying as queer is about forming a community with other queer people, one in which we ensure each other's safety, constantly check each other's politics, and make sure that we don't become poisoned by the pressures of heteronormativity. My queer family is as much celebratory of me as it is challenging of me – in the queer circles I belong to, my attitudes are constantly checked and improved, so that I might practise the most pure and inclusive kind of queer religion possible. Wilayah is the same among Muslims – it's not about controlling each other, but instead about protecting each other, and ensuring our sisters and brothers are not maligned by forces that try to harm and corrupt us. As in the above quotation, it's striking too that the Quran believes masculinity and femininity to be free from actual biology, and more like forces capable of existing within all people – a very queer picture!

During the session, I learnt of an ancient concept in Islam called *ijtihad*. This essentially refers to the circles of critical thinking and independent discussion that for centuries addressed questions in Islam. Until the tenth century, Muslims were encouraged to exercise autonomy of thinking and to contest the Quran, so that each and every Muslim had their own, independent relationship with the text, with the collective readings of Islam generated from many different perspectives. The entire point was to allow a multiplicity of experiences and perspectives to inform the practice of Islam. The Quran, in fact, is much more like a collection of poems than a literal series of commandments; its purposeful ambiguity is intended to encourage a diverse range of interpretations. But, as with everything else in the world, cisgender heterosexual men soon dominated the practice, and *ijtihad* was prohibited in the tenth century, meaning that Islam became more autocratic and restrictive in the way that people understand it to this day. And the passages like *The Story of Lot*, which textually seem far more likely to be warnings against rape and inhospitality, could be co-opted by conservative Islamic practitioners

into an unequivocal condemnation of homosexuality, leading to the kind of religious institutional homophobia that
has scarred my life. It's not Allah who forbade my queer
identity, but the people who ignored the well of alternative
potentials in the Quran.

Since that meeting, I have spent hours and hours trawling
through all the information collated by the queer Muslim
group, and their work has been invaluable in helping me to
find peace in my Islamic heritage. Sufism is a rich and
spiritual sect of Islam that has many affinities with queer
identity. As a queer person, I believe almost dogmatically
in difference, in the idea that every single person is unique,
with their own innate sense of self, and that it is this
difference which brings all of us together as one. Sufism, in
many ways, is based on a similar belief. It's a branch of
Islam in search of a metaphysical and profound personal
dialogue with Allah. In Sufism, every single Muslim has
their own individual relationship with Allah; Allah is not a
singular hegemonic force that controls us all, but something
we can each find individually and on our own terms. Whilst
I had grown up to perceive Islam as ascetic and austere, I
completely missed an entire genealogy of the faith that
directly resonated with me. I had deified the Western
literary greats like Oscar Wilde for their queer magic, and
completely skipped over the writings of Sufists, like
thirteenth-century Persian poet Jalaluddin Rumi, whose
dazzlingly spiritual poems are burning with homoerotic
desire. It was all there the whole time. Just waiting for me.

Prayer methods in Sufism can be wonderfully poetic, and also intrinsically queer. There is a glorious Sufi sect in which men dress in skirts and spin around and dance as a way to fuse their souls with Allah (the infamous whirling dervishes). *YES, THAT'S CORRECT. MALE MUSLIMS WEARING SKIRTS.* So while I'd gone about believing that Allah and every relative of mine was prepared to have me shot for my gender identity, there were actually male Muslims wearing dresses and dancing with Allah – and they actually got *rewarded* for being pious! *I mean, I'm basically doing that every time I perform in drag – maybe it's not so transgressive after all!* I'd spent a lot of my teenage years searching for representations on TV and in film that reflected me, and, although I discovered some beautiful queer characters to connect with, the only thing I found that somewhat resonated with my experience as a queer person of Muslim heritage was *Bend it Like Beckham* (where the queerness in this instance came from a sodding football).

When I learnt about Sufist whirling dervishes, YouTube of all places provided the place where I could more directly see myself. I couldn't believe the footage I was seeing – men, wearing billowing white skirts that would outdo Kim Kardashian on her wedding day, being celebrated by Muslim people in the audience, as they limped their wrists and twirled to the sound of an Imam singing the Quran. Here was a version of drag in the most Islamic context; for the first time ever, I actually identified with Muslims on the screen in front of me, each of whom was searching for meaning through costume, music, and ritual.

I realised that each time I perform in drag, I'm also searching for a transcendental connection with a higher power, channelled through the collective queer energy that comes from the audience. Whenever I get into drag – the quiet ritual of meticulously applying make-up and building a new self – I feel like I did as a young child praying. Islamic prayer is a very charged experience, in which you quietly allow your body to find Allah through movements and mantras. Every time I block out my brows and tell myself in the mirror 'You're fierce', I feel an affinity with these Islamic practices.

Recently, to calm myself before a show, I have been using Muslim prayer poses in my stretches, and it helps me to feel connected and grounded before getting onstage. When I am in my full Arabian get-up in front of an audience, I sometimes like to sing in Arabic, acting as a vessel for the beautiful queer feminine energies in Islam, feeling the spiritual power of what it means to be queer and to have a room of many different people celebrating this. It is a kind of religious experience, a room united in the celebration of difference; when a show goes really well, it gives me a kind of faith. A faith that Allah's plan was for me to twirl onstage in a skirt so that I could eventually find not only myself, but Allah, like many Sufist Muslims had been doing centuries before me.

Whilst this may have been Allah's design for me all along, there are many reasons that this was elusive to me. Ironically, the West – a goal to which I've aspired my entire life – is a key factor. Western colonialism majorly wiped out Sufism across the globe for fear that it was 'secret', 'irrational', and 'dangerous', damaging the more tolerant attitudes within Islam. Conservative laws introduced through colonialism are as much to blame for the regressive policies we see in many Islamic nations. And so the Allah who was really there for me this whole time became obscured by the brutal legacy of western interventions.

I'm not a fully 'practising' Muslim in the traditional sense now. But I have found great peace thinking of Allah as a genderqueer matriarchal protector, a non-binary aquatic being with a 'they' pronoun. They flow through me and encourage me to be different, and to embody all the subatomic contradicting particles that make up who I am.

At the most recent Gay Pride parade in London, I was walking around Oxford Street in an emerald-green snake-like dress that was inspired by a Balmain piece my mum once wore (she usually only wears things once). The parade was a deeply uninspiring and uninviting proposition to me. Corporation after corporation, from Starbucks and Wagamama to Barclays and sodding Coutts paraded their allegiance to the LGBTQIA+ community. *What the fuck have udon noodles and contactless payment ever done to help me with homophobia?* The advertising surrounding the parade boasted gay people who neatly conform to heteronormative ideals, doing respectable jobs, getting married, and raising kids. This isn't to say that such things shouldn't be obtainable, but it gives one the sense that the only thing being lauded is that queer people can now have what straight people have always had, and there is no outward celebration of queer people who do not conform to heteronormative societal ideals. You rarely see the diversity of people who really make up the LGBTQIA+ community in such imagery – for instance drag queens, gender nonconformists, fetishists, and the brave queer people who choose to live a non-normative way of life. Not to mention people of colour, who are barely visible among the gay celebrations. This is partly due to the growing racism within the gay community, highlighted particularly by the co-option of LGBTQIA+ rights from Right-Wing movements, many of whom persuade that immigration from non-Western countries is a threat to gay civil liberties (it's telling that nearly a third of married gay men in Paris voted for Islamophobe incarnate Marine Le Pen in her French presidential election).

As I walked through the parade, I was alarmed by the sheer quantity of white muscular bodies around me, and the overt Eurocentrism of the whole affair. The unashamed deification of capitalist brands gives the parade an intensely secular feel, as if Western capitalism were the saviour of queer people. As if the free market was the reason queer people now have freedom (it isn't – capitalism polices and exploits queer bodies all the time, driving us to aspire to ideals that do not protect the community and which encourage us to compete amongst each other). It was all so unappetising that I decided to leave.

On the walk home, I thought about how much I had revered the West in my life, and how I had thought that the Western establishment was where I so desperately wanted to belong. But all these attempts at belonging brought with them painful exclusion, and diverted me from the many magical things I didn't realise were hidden in my own heritage and faith. I too had been co-opted by Islamophobia, and allowed myself to believe the narrative of Islam as a totalising force of evil. But why is it that even though many Catholic priests have sexually assaulted children, we are still able to imagine Christianity as a bastion of morality? Yes, many Islamic countries have regressive policies – as do some Christian countries – but this doesn't mean that the faith itself is at its core regressive. As with anything, when a thought system becomes instrumentalised and institutionalised, it can lead to extremism and patriarchal governance. When I finally got home, I was happy to be away from the parade, knowing that a rampantly secular gathering of mostly white bodies was not where I belonged.

The next day, however, was one of the most powerful of my life. I attended an event in London called Black Pride, a much-needed antidote to the grossly corporate and apolitical affair of Pride in London, centring queer people of colour, and celebrating a diversity of bodies and identities. Whereas Pride has become a place that presents LGBTQIA+ people within the framework of heteronormative corporate success, Black Pride is a political and inclusive event that gives queer people a truly safe, alternative space, a glorious occasion spread across a park in Vauxhall. I went with a group of friends, including my dear Layla, my majestic drag sister Crystal, and a wonderful queer female friend called Ellie who I love deeply. As we were wandering around, a shy, handsome Arab person moved towards me, telling me that they were aware of my work and were grateful to have seen some queer Arab representation in the media. With a bewitching stare, they gestured for me and my friends to come with them to 'Pride of Arabia'.

We were guided to a hidden pocket of Black Pride, away from the central path that takes you to the main stage, in the corner of a lawn tucked away from the big crowds. I soon found myself among a group of queer Arabs and Muslims, flaunting the costumes of their pasts in true queer glory, many in drag, belly dancing to the Middle Eastern sounds that had raised them (and for some, excluded them). Layla was by my side, as if in that moment our traumatic associations with our heritage were suddenly silenced, and all we felt in front of us was love, solidarity, and beauty. The two runaway Arabs had finally reached their destination.

I didn't think the moment could get any better, but then the rich, powerful sound of Umm Kulthum's voice came through the speakers, and I was directly communicating with that little Amrou on the couch in Bahrain with Mama, assuring them that eventually, it was all going to be OK. It was going to be better than OK – it would be glorious.

I breathed in the colourful display of bodies, all intertwining together, each and every one of us fusing our heritage with our queer identities. My eyes closed, I spun around like a whirling dervish, feeling a loving, non-binary Allah soothing all my wounds. I felt as if I was inside my teenage aquarium, swimming in a magical potion that blended all of the fragmented parts of my identity. Like the quantum subatomic particles that make up our universe, I was finally able to inhabit all the different facets of who I am in a single moment. When the Umm Kulthum song finished, I got out my phone and I sent a message: 'Mama, I love you.'

ACKNOWLEDGEMENTS

Firstly, I would like to thank Kitty Laing, my extraordinary agent, who believed in me right at the beginning of my career, even when I struggled to believe in myself. Thank you from the bottom of my heart for emboldening me to be the best queen I can be, for teaching me my worth, for supporting me through the good times and the bad, for all the life-changing opportunities, and for taking care of me. I am forever grateful to you, both as an agent and as a dear friend.

Thank you to my phenomenal book agents at United, Jon Elek & Millie Hoskins, for pushing me and testing me to create the best material I could, for fighting my corner and supporting me even when I thought I couldn't do it. This book would not have been possible without you, and your support and kindness has kept me going. Thank you to my whole team at United Agents for always having my back, the glorious Isaac Storm, the majestic Katya Balfour-Lynn, the wonderful Giles Smart, Jennifer Thomas, Rosa Schierenberg and Frances Greenfield.

Thank you to my exceptional editor Anna Kelly, for guiding me through this emotionally tumultuous process with remarkable calm and wisdom, for your incredibly astute notes at every stage, for taking a chance on me as an author, and for being so patient throughout (especially during my breakdowns ... for which I am sorry!). I am indebted to the whole team at 4th Estate; Helen, David, Patrick, Matt, Liv, Fran, Paul – you really are the most overqualified and incredible team a queen could ask for, and I am very lucky to be with you. Thank you also to Sophie Wilson, for your invaluable advice and support on my initial proposal – you really helped me to shape what this book could be, and I'm deeply grateful to you.

Thank you to Lettice Franklin, for giving me the confidence to write this book all the way at the start, for advising me and supporting me throughout, and for being one of the kindest and most generous people there ever was. Our 'one-on-ones' mean everything to me, and your friendship is one of the greatest joys of my life.

Thank you to Russell T Davies, for being an exceptional mentor, a fiercely loyal and honest friend, and for pushing me to the best of my ability. You've challenged me to be a better creative and a better person, and I feel so lucky to know you.

ACKNOWLEDGEMENTS

Thank you to my teachers Luke Skrebowski & Karolina Watras for inspiring me and opening up my mind so vividly. I hope you know what a profound effect your teachings had on me.

Thank you so much to my brother Ramy, for your unconditional support and your amazing heart. I don't tell you enough how much I love and respect you.

Thank you to Harry Carr, my angelic unicorn, for being such a ray of light, hope, support, and inspiration. I am so lucky to have you in my life, and my world is a brighter place because you are in it. I love you unconditionally.

Thank you to Ellie Kendrick, for being family, for growing with me, for supporting me through everything, and for teaching me so much. You are an uncommonly good person, and I don't know where I'd be without you.

Thank you to Matthew Knott. I cannot believe that it was pure luck that brought you into my life. You have supported and enriched me in more ways than I can express. Thank you for being one of the most loyal and kind friends I've ever had, for your constant wisdom, and for all the things we've learned together.

Thank you to Amnah Hafez – you are a sister to me, and a complete gift. I am so grateful to you on so many levels, for healing me and making me smile like no-one else. We were always meant to be together.

Thank you to Tom Rasmussen – what can I say? You are my queer sister till the very end, and a constant source of joy, support and inspiration. You make me feel stronger every day, and I hope you know just how extraordinary you are. I feel so enriched by what we have together, and look forward to my queer horizon forever expanding with you. The same goes for you, Hatty – our queer discoveries have shaped me and guided me, and I feel so blessed to have someone as radically magical as you in my life. I love you.

Thank you to Denim, my first queer family. You saved me. Shugsy, your purity and kindness is a treasure, and you can genuinely make me laugh like nobody else (and shout out to the wonderful Jessie Wyld and our iconic tinnies!). Charlie – you have creatively pushed me and supported me my entire career, you've taught me so much, and your eccentricity has never stopped giving me joy. Guy, thank you for being one of the most uncommonly loyal friends there is out there – I cherish it, and am so grateful.

Thank you to Polly Stenham, for your fiercely supportive friendship, and for being there during some of the hardest times in my life. You are an extraordinarily generous friend, and the understanding we share is rare and sacred.

Thank you to Victoria Sin, for teaching me to take up space, for opening my eyes, expanding my world, for making me feel safe and seen, and for inspiring me. You are a one in a trillion, and our time together has taught me so much and filled up my heart.

Thank you to Amelia Abraham, for being a truly loyal friend, for always giving the best advice, and for making me see the funny side of things. You are an extraordinarily loving person, and I am so grateful for our friendship.

Thank you from the bottom of my heart to Bex – we've shared so much emotionally, and I count you as family. Thank you for always being honest with me and for forever leading with your heart – I adore you and love you. You too Niko – we've gone through the world together, and so much of who I've become was because you were there with me. Thank you Sophie Crawford, for being such a good-hearted, generous, and truly hilarious friend. You are a wonder, and your talents always inspire me. Thank you Eve Hedderwick Turner, for every dinner where we've shared our work and supported each other. And to Check – I don't know how I would have survived Cambridge without you; some of the times we shared together have been the happiest of my life.

Thank you to Marina Diamandis, for teaching me to love myself, for all we've shared emotionally, and for inspiring me as an artist. You are a complete jewel, and I feel absurdly lucky to have you as a friend. Thank you to Florence Welch, for your always healing poetry and incredible generosity of heart.

Thank you to Amia & Sophie – you have both stretched my mind and touched my heart in a multitude of ways, and I only wish we saw more of each other. You're incredible.

Thank you to my Camberwell Queer Crew – Tricia & Briony, you've made me feel like I've had a home, and I always feel giddy happy whenever I'm with your family. Thank you to Savannah James-Bayly, for being my queer creative partner these past few years – they have meant a tremendous amount to me, and I cannot wait to continue growing and making space with you. Our bond is so precious, and I am so grateful for it.

Thank you so much to Mary Burke and to Phil Canning, for always supporting me, making me laugh, and for taking me in at Christmas. Your beautiful family are a complete joy.

Thank you to my oldest friends for growing up with me and always showing me love – Hannah Wardroper, Edmund Weeks, Cornelio Brennand.

Thank you to all the extraordinary queer people and people of colour who have given me hope, fight and meaning, even when you didn't know you were doing it – Travis Alabanza, Nadia Latif, Candice Carty-Williams, Juno Roche, Shon Faye, Huw Lemmey, Shay Shay, Chiyo Gomes, Umber Ghauri, Munroe Bergdorf, Kuchenga, Paris Lees, Kennedy Walker, CN Lester, BBZ, Juno Dawson, Jamie Windust, Alok Vaid-Menon, Michael Walker, Farhana Bhula, Sarah Brocklehurst, Matimba Kabalika, Jules Kelly, Caitlin Benedict, Arlie Addington, Stephen Dunn, Riz Ahmed, Riyadh Khalaf, The Vixen, Nina West, Sasha Velour, Shea Couleé, Joel Price, Simon Amstell, Daniel Chandler, Phyll Opoku-Gyimah, Max Cocking, Stephen Dunn, Sadhbh O' Sullivan, Marcelo Ceatano, Marco Alessi, Matthew James Morgan, Dionne Edwards, Joy Gharoro-

ACKNOWLEDGEMENTS

Akpojotor, Ash Sarkar, Owen Jones, Faiza Shaheen and Koby Adom, the list could go on.

Thank you so much to my psychotherapist, Daniel, for teaching me about … me. I owe you a lot. And finally, thank you to my mother and father for all your sacrifices. We've gone through hell and back, but the love we have for each other has never faltered, and I wouldn't be the person I am now without you. I love you.